TOILET
TRAINING
WITHOUT
TANTRUMS

OTHER BOOKS BY JOHN ROSEMOND

TOILET
TRAINING
WITHOUT
TANTRUMS

JOHN ROSEMOND

Andrews McMeel
Publishing, LLC
Kansas City • Sydney • London

To the many parents who were willing to contribute their stories to this project so that other parents could benefit from their mistakes and successes

Andrews McMeel Publishing, LLC
an Andrews McMeel Universal company
1130 Walnut Street, Kansas City, Missouri 64106

www.andrewsmcmeel.com

12 13 14 15 16 MLT 10 9 8 7 6 5 4 3 2 1

ISBN: 978-1-4494-1848-9

Library of Congress Control Number: 2011944585

ATTENTION: SCHOOLS AND BUSINESSES
Andrews McMeel books are available at quantity discounts with bulk purchase for educational, business, or sales promotional use. For information, please e-mail the Andrews McMeel Publishing Special Sales Department: specialsales@amuniversal.com

ACKNOWLEDGMENTS

I want to express my appreciation to:

- Debbie Wickwire at Thomas Nelson Publishers for graciously returning to me the rights to this book.

- My agent, Steve Laube, for providing a great deal of encouragement and direction, ongoing.

- My good buddy, Don Jacobsen, for sharing his knowledge of and expertise in self-publishing and his helpful comments and suggestions on the text.

- The many parents (and their children) who contributed stories of toilet-training failure and toilet-training success.

- My loving wife, Willie, for her patience and support throughout the project.

I especially want to thank Diane Kottakis, who during the years she served as the resident toilet-training expert on my Web site helped many, many parents achieve toilet-training success. Diane wrote an initial rough draft of the book and contributed much of the historical research found in Chapters 1 and 2.

I can only pray that I've made no glaring errors. If I have, I take full responsibility for them.

CONTENTS

READER'S GUIDE

I tried my best to keep this book short. After all, I am claiming that toilet training is a simple, uncomplicated process. However, I also think that a historical overview of toilet-training advice and practice helps put into proper perspective the general brouhaha that now surrounds the subject. To paraphrase philosopher George Santayana, those who do not understand the recent past are doomed to repeat it.

Chapters 1 and 2 provide that historical overview. I think it will be helpful for parents who are about to embark on this Great Adventure to know how the simple process of teaching a child to use the toilet became so completely messed up. But if you want to risk doom, you are free to skip the history and dive straight into the how-to material, Chapters 3 and 4. If you are struggling with a child three or older who is not yet fully trained and may even be refusing to use the toilet, Chapter 5 is your ticket. But please, regardless, read Chapters 3 and 4 first.

In Chapter 6, I lay out the pros and cons of what is being called infant elimination training or elimination communication (I prefer the former). Chapter 7 deals with bedwetting and what is erroneously called night training. Chapter 8 really isn't a chapter. It's what's known as a coda.

If you're in a hurry to get this over with, or you've already experienced as much difficulty as you can take, read Chapters 3, 4, and 5. If you're interested in the big picture and you're not Type A, read it all.

That's it in a nutshell. Happy toilet training!

INTRODUCTION

In 2000, I added a question-and-answer feature to the members' side of my Web site at www.rosemond.com. Of the first thousand questions submitted, close to 250—one in four—dealt with some aspect of toilet training. Parents wrote in about children who were completely oblivious to the presence of a potty, were still having frequent accidents after three to six months of training, or just plain refused to sit. If my membership was any indication, toilet training was the single most vexing, anxiety-arousing, stress-inducing, infuriating, guilt-ridden parenting problem of the preschool years.

Upon close examination, I discovered that in nearly every problem situation, parents had waited to begin training until well after their children had turned two. I also could not help but notice that in many instances, parents reported that they had waited until a child was two-and-one-half, three, or even older because that's what their pediatrician had told them to do.

Intrigued, I called a few pediatrician friends—ones who advised training before or around the second birthday—and asked them why so many of their colleagues were dispensing this very bad advice to parents. The answer, in every case: That's what pediatrician and parenting book author T. Berry Brazelton advises, and his advice has become the pediatric standard when it comes to toilet training.

I'd met Brazelton in the mid-1980s while attending one of his seminars and knew that central to his toilet-training philosophy was the concept of "readiness signs," a set of specific behavioral indicators that a child was sufficiently mature—physically, intellectually, and emotionally—and could therefore control his eliminations, understand the process, and handle its supposed psychological rigors. In fact, said seminar had made a convert out of me. For years, I chanted the readiness-signs mantra in my newspaper column, books, and public presentations. During that time, however, I began researching the history of toilet training in America, talking to American parents who had toilet trained children before age two, and talking to parents from other countries where pre-two training was the norm. I slowly came to the conclusion that the concept of readiness was largely hogwash. In 1999, in my nationally syndicated parenting column, I ate crow for having lent credibility to the notion:

Q *As for the matter of readiness signs, I am now convinced this is so much psychobabble. I apologize for ever giving parents the impression that toilet training is a delicate issue that must be approached with a keen eye for signals from the child that he/she is psychologically capable of dealing with the requirements of the process.*

A At the same time, I began advocating a method of training that I called "Naked and $75." In part, I'm sure, because of the catchiness of the term, the media began giving me my fifteen minutes of fame. In a page 1 story, *The New York Times* favorably compared my toilet-training philosophy with Brazelton's. I was invited to guest on *Good Morning America*, *20/20*, and NBC's *Later Today*. On one national talk show, I debated a California pediatrician and Brazelton disciple who insisted that training a child younger than two required undue "force" and was likely to result in great frustration, angst, and long-term psychological harm. During the exchange, I speculated that my opponent, being of approximately the same age as me, was probably trained before age two. I asked, "Can you tell us what long-term harm you suffered as a result?" She looked like the proverbial deer in the headlights. After a moment of surprised silence, she stammered that indeed, her mother had told her she'd been trained at eighteen months. However, she quickly added that the person who was actually trained was her mother, not her. She conveniently avoided answering the most important aspect of my question: How had "early" (in fact, eighteen months was pretty much the norm fifty years ago) training caused her long-term psychological harm? Needless to say, she would have been unable to identify any such harm. My point was that objective evidence of what Brazelton and his disciples are claiming is completely, utterly lacking. His claims qualify as hogwash.

I think Brazelton is a well-intentioned man who has caused a great deal of harm. With his very bad toilet-training advice—I call it toilet-babble—he tossed a huge monkey wrench into American parenting. His advice transformed something simple and straightforward into something complicated; something down-to-earth into something supposedly fraught with apocalyptic psychological ramifications. For hundreds of years, toilet training represented liberation for mothers. They looked forward to it. Since Brazelton began spreading his bad news, it has become the parenting equivalent of a triple root canal without anesthesia.

Here are the facts about toilet training:

- It is a fundamentally simple process, not, as pediatrician and author William Sears claims, "highly complex."[1] He means it is complex for the child, but this definitely implies that toilet training involves lots of complexity for the parent, as well, that she must be properly attuned to a host of practical and psychological details and be constantly on her proverbial toes.

- Toilet training is no more fraught with psychological ramifications than is teaching a child to feed himself with a spoon or tie his shoes.

- It's easier—much easier, in fact—to toilet train a child before his or her second birthday than after.

- Toilet training's window of opportunity is widest between eighteen and twenty-four months of age.

- There is no objective evidence—none—that children trained before age two, even before eighteen months, are likely to suffer psychological stress, much less harm.

- The concept of "readiness" is hokum, bunk, hogwash, frogfeathers, claptrap, rubbish. In fact, it's a scam. Who profits from the resulting delays in training? Disposable-diaper manufacturers and mental-health professionals.

- Managed properly, toilet training requires very little involvement on the part of the parent. In fact, the more involved a parent is in the process, the more resistant the child is likely to become.

- There is no "luck" involved in early toilet training, and children who are trained early are not necessarily "easy" children.

- A bad toilet-training experience may set the stage for ongoing problems in the parent–child relationship. Likewise, a good toilet-training experience sets the stage for continued success in the parent–child relationship.

- Today's parents are likely to receive better toilet-training advice from their parents and grandparents (for sure the latter) than from pediatricians and psychologists.

My intention in writing this book is to help set matters straight concerning toilet training. To do so, I will state my case in terms of facts rather than theories and unproven speculations. I intend to draw aside the curtain of mystification and reveal toilet training for the uncomplicated process it is. This radical (by today's standards) contention is supported by the fact that your great-grandmother, and perhaps even your grandmother, and perhaps even your mother, toilet trained her children (you, perhaps?) in a matter of days—certainly no more than a few weeks—and did so before their second birthdays.

The premodern mom did not analyze readiness signs or agonize over the psychological implications of her approach. She simply told her child that he was no longer going to wear diapers; he was going to begin using the toilet. Period. She gave him the support he needed to learn what to do, and she steered an unwavering course. If after some success he had a relapse, she did not question her purpose. Nor did she question his ability. She accepted that his learning was going to involve some missteps (as is the case with learning any new task), and when they occurred, she took them in purposeful stride. It is my greatest hope that this book will help today's parents reclaim that confidence and sense of purpose.

A WISE GRANDMOTHER WRITES: I am the mother of four and grandmother of two, all of whom have been trained by their second birthdays. I put them on the potty at intervals during the day: after waking, after eating, after nap, and whenever they had been dry for a period of time. They would sit and play with a toy or look at a book. They were completely trained by their second birthdays. It was a completely natural process with no grief for them or me. Training them before age two also saved my husband and me lots of money! What is wrong with parents these days? It is like common sense has gone out the window. I appreciate the way you try to set these modern parents straight!

I'm also going to reveal the arcane secrets of "Naked and $75" (N75), which are not so arcane at all. Nor is N75 even new. After I explained it in several newspaper columns published between 1999 and 2002, several older women whose parents had immigrated to America from Europe, Asia, and Africa informed me that when it came time for them to train their children, their mothers told them how to do it. Their mothers' method was pretty much what I thought had been the product of my own genius. I should have known. After all, there is nothing new under the sun.[2]

After opening up the members' side of www.rosemond.com and after answering several hundred toilet-training questions, I began to feel that if I had to answer one more I might begin to lose my mind. About this time, Diane Kottakis—whom I had met at a speaking engagement—contacted me about her experiences with toilet training her first two children. With her first child, a girl, she had taken Brazelton's advice and waited until her daughter was three to initiate training. The child saw no benefit to using the toilet and defied all of Diane's best efforts to persuade her to do so. Using N75, Diane began training her second, also a girl, at seventeen months. Several relatively stress-free months later, the child was completely trained and was even using the toilet in public places. In fact, Diane had trained her firstborn and her secondborn at the same time. With the former, she used the same advice I give to parents of older children who resist using the toilet (see Chapter 5); with the latter, she used N75.

It occurred to me that perhaps, having experienced the consequences of both Brazelton's readiness approach and Rosemond's N75, Diane was as qualified as anyone to mentor other parents through toilet training. After all, this is not something that requires professional credentials. So I asked her to serve as the resident toilet-training expert on my Web site. Much to my delight, she agreed. Since then, Diane has helped many grateful parents train their children before their second birthdays, and has mentored many equally grateful parents—of older children, mostly—through all manner of toilet-training quandaries. She did a good amount of the historical research found in Chapters 1 and 2, and several of the success stories contained herein are the result of her work with parents through my Web site.

Diane and I have discovered that when parents understand the rationale and how-to of N75, they are able to approach toilet training with confidence and almost always report quick success. This book is intended to empower you, the reader, and help you bring about that same success. An ever-increasing number of parents know and believe that toilet training by age twenty-four months is not only realistic but also desirable and beneficial for everyone in the family. Many of these psychobabble-liberated parents were excited to share their experiences for the benefit of those reading this book. I am most grateful for their wisdom and experience.

A HAPPY MOTHER WRITES: Like a lot of parents nowadays, we kept waiting and waiting for that magic moment when our son would decide, "It's time, I'm ready now!" One day, my husband and I looked at one another and a light bulb came on. Our twenty-three-month-old son already talked in sentences, learned quickly, remembered little details about everything, and loved challenges. "Um, honey, if he is all of these things, why are we still letting him pee and poop in his pants?" Eureka! He was toilet trained that very week—after we made the decision that he was ready.

If at this point you are exclaiming, "Woe is me and woe is my child!" because your child is older than two—much older, even—and is still wearing "Little Depends," take heart. As attested by many parents, "Naked and $75" works with children older than two. I'm even going to describe how to triumph over the worst-case scenario: an older child who puts up a fight or acts like she's toilet training challenged. No potty jam is too big for Pottyman's potty plan!

This book will provide you with not only a new perspective on toilet training but a new perspective on parenting itself. I am convinced that the toilet training model contained herein is simply a model for old-fashioned good parenting. As such, successful early toilet training will set a positive precedent for you as a parent, a precedent that will prove beneficial for years to come. Thanks for giving Diane and me this opportunity to spread the good news!

ANOTHER HAPPY MOTHER WRITES: Thanks so much to you and Diane for all the wonderful information on your Web site. It's made me a more relaxed parent, which makes life so much more enjoyable. I recently had great success with "Naked and $75" for my twenty-four-month-old daughter (trained in five days). Most important to her success was for me to have the right attitude, for her to have a potty available close by, and to tell her and show by example what needed to be done and then let her do it on her own! My friends who used the let-the-child-decide-when-to-potty-train method (and had kids in diapers at almost four years old) are amazed.

A BRIEF HISTORY
OF TOILET TRAINING
IN AMERICA

In scientific terms, toilet training in America has been characterized by entropy, which means that, like all systems in the universe, it has steadily deteriorated over time. In political terms, recommended toilet training practice over the past hundred years (since "experts" began pontificating on the subject) has moved from the extreme right to the extreme left, from a state of rigid conservatism to a state of sloppy, sentimental liberalism. Once parent centered, it is now child centered. It has gone from being down-to-earth to having its proverbial head in the clouds, from being a purely practical matter to something dominated by psychological theory. In the same span of time, toilet training has devolved from something parents simply did without fanfare to being the single most stressful parenting event of the preschool years. One hundred years ago, a mother sought guidance from *her* mother when it came to toilet training; today, parents (today's warm and fuzzy Dad wants in on the act) seek advice from psychologists, pediatricians, and various parenting experts, including me. Grandma gave good advice. Toilet training advice coming from the professional quarter has gone from bad to worse to downright wrong.

DONE AT ONE

The first expert advice on toilet training—or "elimination training," as it was then called—appeared in 1914 in *Infant Care,* a free pamphlet published periodically thereafter by the U.S. Government. Table 1 summarizes its toilet training advice from inception until 1951.

TABLE 1. Toilet Training Advice from the U.S. Government *Infant Care* Pamphlet, 1914–1951

1914: Bowel training to start by three months. The mother should use "the utmost gentleness. . . . Scolding and punishment will only frighten the child and destroy the natural impulses, while laughter will . . . relax the muscles and promote an easy movement."

1921: Bowel training to begin as soon as possible and completed by twelve months. Mentions using a soap-stick suppository for a few days in order to facilitate a bowel movement and create a habit. No mention of laughter or gentleness, and no warning against scolding.

1929: Claims that "almost any baby can be trained so that there are no more soiled diapers to wash after he is six to eight months old." The daily routine is completely by the clock.

1938: Bowel training to start as early as six months and be completed by twelve months, but the approach is now child centered. Instead, parents are told to "observe the baby's own rhythm in selecting the time of day for a bowel movement."

1942 AND 1945: Bowel training to start at eight to ten months and finish in six weeks, although some accidents are considered normal. Bladder training to start right after bowel training is finished.

1951: Bowel training to start between eighteen and twenty-four months. First mention of nervous-system development playing a part in training. Parents told not to put child on toilet more than two or three times per day and also not to interrupt his play.

Excluding the liberalized 1951 edition, note the emphasis on the mother's adherence to a rigid, time-bound training routine. Today's parent may scoff at the notion that a child can be successfully trained by one year, if not sooner, but the historical evidence is clear: Training before one year was once the norm. For that to be accomplished, significant diligence on the part of the child's mother was needed, a diligence that has led contemporary pundits to dismiss the premodern mother's success by claiming that *she* was the person trained, not her child. If that means that she had to be highly organized, fastidiously attentive, and single-minded in her determination, then indeed, the premodern mother was "trained" in the sense of being self-disciplined where her role in the process was concerned.

But for parents to train a child to *any* new task requires that they be organized, attentive, and focused. In other words, for parents to discipline a child to any new set of expectations requires that they be disciplined in their approach; therefore, the attempt to dismiss the premodern mother's success on this basis is in vain. She began toilet training her child before one year for three primary reasons: first, cloth manufactured diapers were beyond the financial means of the average family, and therefore "diapers" were usually improvised and very inconvenient; second, the fact that the premodern mother's work was almost literally never done rendered it vital that she make her child as independent of her as quickly as possible; and third, although the Victorian era was officially over in 1901, its influence on such things as the general cultural attitude toward bodily functions (i.e., unmentionable) was considerable until the 1960s.

The advice found in the few available pre-Spock (1946) child-rearing books was similar to that in *Infant Care,* but most of these experts accepted that with most children the process would not be fully accomplished until sometime between eighteen and twenty-four months. Table 2 summarizes professional toilet training advice from the 1920s until the start of World War II, after which Dr. Benjamin Spock, America's first celebrity pediatrician, arrived on the scene.

TABLE 2. Toilet Training Advice from
Various U.S. Child Care Books, 1925–1940

GESELL, 1925: Bowel training should begin around eighteen months, bladder training around twenty-four months.

GRIFFITH, 1926: Education can begin before three months. Complete control acquired by twenty-four months, needing a diaper only at night, if at all.

WATSON, 1928: Start training via conditioned response as early as three weeks. Bladder training completed during day by fifteen months old, dry at night is possible at twenty-four months old.

FEAGRE, 1930: Bowel training can start at six weeks, with most having one bowel movement a day at twelve months. Start bladder training at twelve months and complete by twenty-four months.

ALDRICH AND ALDRICH, 1938: Condemns the use of suppositories, maintaining that their use overrides the innate internal reflex of the child and is thus detrimental to training.

GESELL, 1940: Introduces notion that learning to control elimination is part of a larger developmental process. For example, says that at fifteen months the child is capable of telling parents when he's wet and may begin to wake up dry from naps. Generally recommends that training commence around eighteen months.

One item of note is that both *Infant Care* and the first wave of child care professionals recommended that bowel training *precede* bladder training. It was once taken for granted that bowel training was more easily accomplished than bladder training—perhaps because it's easier for the parent to predict a bowel movement—and was the latter's prerequisite. Indeed, experience has led me to conclude that many of the problems today's parents encounter with bowel training are due to the fact that, with rare exception, they do not start it until *after* bladder training has been accomplished, sometimes well after. I find that children learn both processes more readily if they are presented simultaneously.

FREUD OR FRAUD?

As Tables 1 and 2 reveal, a shift in attitude toward toilet training began occurring in the 1930s, away from the rigidity earlier espoused and toward a general agreement that the child's active participation, or at least some appreciation of the child's individuality, was important. Professionals also began recommending a more relaxed approach rather than adherence to an obsessively inflexible schedule. In large part, this trend reflected the influence of Viennese psychiatrist Sigmund Freud's theories of human development. Freud believed that during a child's early years (roughly corresponding to what today are called the preschool years) he proceeds through oral, anal, and Oedipal psychosexual stages, each marked by an important event that, if not handled properly by the child's parents, will cause psychological problems and eventually culminate in adult neurosis or even psychosis.

Concerning Freud's anal phase, which corresponds roughly to the second and third years of life, the critical event was toilet training. Freud's hypothesis was that if toilet training was done too early, too late, or punitively, the child's personality would become fixated at that stage of development, ultimately yielding an adult with an "anal" personality characterized by compulsive neatness, stinginess, and stubbornness—think Felix of *The Odd Couple*. In his 1908 essay "Character and Anal Eroticism," Freud also posited that fixation in the anal stage could also explain homosexuality, paranoia, chronic constipation, and a preoccupation with money.[3] Obviously, Freud believed toilet training to be a primary determinant of personality development. (In fact, Freud seems to have been a tad fixated on the issue of toilet training. I'll bet his bathroom was the neatest, cleanest room in his house.)

Despite the fact that Freud's ideas eventually attained popularity and continue to influence a number of psychiatrists and psychologists, not one of his theories has withstood the test of dispassionate scientific scrutiny. No objective, unbiased scientific investigation—and quite a number have been conducted since 1926—has found any correlation between adult personality characteristics and toilet training. Stated simply, Freud's ideas are pure malarkey.

Psychological historian Hans Eysenck accurately called Freud a "genius not of science but of propaganda," whose place is not, as Freud himself egotistically claimed, with Copernicus and Darwin but with Hans Christian Andersen, the Brothers Grimm, and other tellers of fairy tales.[4] Nonetheless, Freud's ideas continue to exert a powerful influence on popular and professional notions of child care and child development. For example, the term *anal personality* is commonly used today to smear people who like their personal environments to be neat, clean, and orderly. As we will see, Freud's nonsense has exerted significant influence on the advice dispensed by none other than the well-intentioned architect of America's toilet-training woes, pediatrician T. Berry Brazelton.

In the 1940s, social scientists began conducting studies designed to bring to light negative aspects of what they considered "early" toilet-training practices (before eighteen months). Invariably, these researchers annulled their own results by starting with faulty premises, many of which were derived from Freud's theories. In 1942, for example, one researcher attempted to prove that severe emotional disturbance in many children could be traced back to coercive toilet training. The problem was that she regarded practices that were then the norm as "premature, overactive, and destructive." Having biased her definitions, she found the connection she was looking for and was able therefore to conclude that, indeed, most emotionally disturbed children had been trained with force. She conveniently failed to mention that, by her standard, most emotionally healthy children of the time had been similarly trained. Other researchers quickly recognized the fallacy in her argument and debunked her conclusions. Nonetheless, in *Toilet Training the Brazelton Way* (2004), Dr. T. Berry Brazelton cites this researcher's work to support his contention that the attempt to train a child before age two is almost certainly incompatible with the child's ability level, requires force (i.e., coercion), and is therefore potentially harmful.

SPOCK SPEAKS

Dr. Benjamin Spock first published *The Common Sense Book of Baby and Child Care* in 1946. It became an instant classic. Contrary to popular myth, Spock's original child-rearing philosophy cannot accurately be described as permissive. His advice on most parenting issues, including discipline, was consistent with both tradition and prevailing popular opinion, neither of which was permissive in the least. For example, although he refrained from actually recommending spankings, Spock thought they were preferable to long-winded parental diatribes. Although he did not specifically mention the four words, it's obvious he had no problem with a parent saying "Because I said so."

Concerning toilet training, Spock told parents they could begin as soon as a baby could sit up on his own (thus, well before the first birthday), but he also said it was perfectly all right to start later. He said that regardless of when a parent decided to start training, the most important elements were the parent's attitude and approach *during the child's second year*. Spock condemned the use of the enemas and suppositories (recommended by some earlier writers on the subject) and warned against engaging in a power struggle with the child. He preached patience and understanding while recommending that parents approach training with a "casual and friendly" attitude. Good advice, overall. But then, with one afterthought, Spock kicked off the wrong-headed notion that if left to his own devices, a child will train himself on schedule: "If you want to be completely natural, you can leave bowel training almost entirely up to your baby . . . [who] will probably take himself to the toilet before he is two years old."

Without specifically recommending it, Spock told parents it was okay to be fairly passive concerning bladder training, as well; that without much if any parental action, a child would be urinating in the toilet no later than age two-and-one-half. For mothers not willing to leave it up to their children, he coined the first-ever readiness sign (though he didn't call it such): the regular ability of the child to stay dry for two hours at a stretch.

Spock's intention was to help parents approach toilet training with a relaxed attitude, which was good, especially considering the rigid approach many professionals had previously recommended. Unfortunately, he also gave permission to parents to leave training almost completely up to their children. He surely had no idea that others would take his aside concerning self-training and ultimately extend it to justify the wearing of diapers by children age three and older.

Shortly after the first publication of Spock's book, noted child psychologist and pediatrician Arnold Gesell came out strongly against bowel and bladder training during infancy. He explained bowel and bladder control as "involuntary mechanisms into which voluntary control is incorporated" and therefore dependent on a certain level of nervous-system maturity, proposing that most children do not reach that milestone until sometime between eighteen and twenty-four months.[5] Gesell's assertion flew in the face of fact: Before his writings, many, many children had been successfully bowel and bladder trained before eighteen months. In fact, although this is certainly not the norm today, a significant number of parents have reported to Diane and me that their children were successfully trained well before eighteen months using "Naked and $75." Please keep in mind that I believe toilet training's window of opportunity is open widest between eighteen and twenty-four months. In that regard, I agree with Gesell. However, I don't agree that a child's nervous system is not sufficiently mature until then. There's no solid evidence to support that contention.

A HAPPY MOTHER PRAISES HER VERY WISE MOTHER-IN-LAW: My old-fashioned Chinese mother-in-law thought we were wrong to wait until our first child, a boy, was at least twenty-four months old to start toilet training, so she took it upon herself to begin training him at sixteen months. She adhered to a consistent routine, and he took to it almost instantly. It truly amazed me how little drama there was. I will never again doubt the wisdom of my no-nonsense elders.

From the early 1950s on, the notion that "readiness" played a part in successful toilet training steadily grew. In his 1968 revision of *Baby and Child Care,* for example, Spock—whose overall parenting philosophy had moved in a more permissive direction over the previous twenty-two years—had expanded his number of readiness signs for bowel training from one to five:

- The child is proud of his bowel movements.

- He begins to take joy in giving things to others.

- His mother's approval is important to him.

- He is fascinated with putting things in containers.

- He warns of an impending bowel movement.

The reader may notice that Spock did away entirely with his first readiness sign—the regular ability to stay dry for two hours—and came up with five new ones. In addition, whereas his first sign pertained to bladder control, his five new signs pertained to bowel control. However, it is significant to note that the "new" Spock somewhat paradoxically recommended that toilet training commence by eighteen months irrespective of readiness signs, pointing out that the child would be "likely to pick up the idea more quickly at this age." Even though he fell more and more under the sway of psychobabble, Spock's common sense continued to prevail.

Unfortunately, by introducing a list of readiness indicators, Spock began to soil the waters of toilet training. From this point, the matter of readiness only became more and more confusing. Most interesting, however, is the fact that Spock rightly observed that using or not using diapers was a strong statement in and of itself and recommended the latter:

Q *To continue to put diapers on a child who is gaining control is an expression of lack of confidence. A diaper invites wetting and soiling.*[6]

A I couldn't agree more! In fact, having the child run naked during training is central to N75, which is actually derived from the very simple, straightforward approach used by mothers worldwide for hundreds if not thousands of years and still widely used in many nonindustrialized cultures.

For the most part, Spock also believed that commencement of toilet training was the parents' decision, not something you ask the child's permission for or wait for the child to initiate. Again, I agree. He encouraged parents to continue with training in the face of resistance from the child. Once more, I agree. Interestingly enough, Spock also recognized that parents who tend to be avid consumers of parent education materials may be putting themselves at a distinct disadvantage. He noted that in one of the clinics in the medical school in which he taught, the parents who had the greatest success with toilet training were those without college degrees or interest in psychology. Their children tended to be trained before their second birthdays, he noted, without struggle or harm to their personalities. Along the same lines, I've made numerous public statements to the effect that parents who think too much tend to create unnecessary problems for themselves and their children.

Obviously, Spock did not intend for his five readiness indicators to be anything more than general markers for parents who needed more than intuition to know when to start training. He had no idea that the next significant potty pundit, Brazelton, whose star was already ascending in 1968, would eventually extend readiness to mean that a parent should do exactly what Spock recommended against: Stop at every sign of resistance and put the child back in diapers.

Despite the gradual liberalization of toilet-training advice from 1914 on, most children before the 1960s were fully bowel and bladder trained by age two. In 1935, an informal survey found that most parents began bowel training before the first birthday, and that it was successfully completed by fourteen months. By 1946, the average age of completion was around eighteen months. A decade later, research conducted by social scientists at Harvard and Stanford Universities was published in *Patterns of Child Rearing* (1957), which became a text used in many university child psychology and child development programs. Of the mothers in Harvard's study, presumably representing a cross-section of American parents, nearly half began bowel training before nine months, with the average age of initiation being eleven months. By age twenty-four months, 80 percent of the children in the study had been successfully toilet trained, defined as accident free for one month.[7] In effect, just two generations ago, 80 percent of American children were accident free by age twenty-three months.

AND THEN ALONG CAME DISPOSABLES

After being invented in 1946, the disposable diaper did not become common and affordable until the early 1970s. In no time, the cloth diaper went the way of buggy whips. Mothers enjoyed the ease of disposables, including the freedom from having to wash out cloth diapers, which often had to be hand washed before they could be run through a washing machine. As a result, moms gradually became less and less motivated to toilet train before their children's second birthdays. That played right into the hands of readiness advocates such as pediatrician T. Berry Brazelton (who served for a time as media spokesperson for Pampers and chairman of the Pampers Parenting Institute).

Unfortunately, the drawbacks of disposables outweigh their advantages. When diapers were wet or soiled, they sagged, signaling that they were full. Disposables are engineered so that they rarely sag, which means parents are less likely to be aware of their children's bowel and bladder habits. When children wore cloth diapers, and those diapers became wet or soiled, they were uncomfortable. Children wanted out of them. Not so with disposables. All this adds to the fact that disposables have turned something that was once drudgery into something that is a minor inconvenience at worst. This has significantly reduced the incentive for parents to train as early as possible.

The readiness camp believes that disposable diapers should be used freely during training, and this idea is now being supported in some professional publications. For example, an article in the highly influential journal *Pediatrics* stated that "emphasis on whether a child passes stool in the toilet or in a diaper is secondary," and that giving the child the option takes the pressure off everyone.[8]

All I have to say about that is we're talking about *toilet* training, not *diaper* training. The goal is to *eliminate* diapers. I can think of few things more confusing to a child through this important process than being told, "We want you to use the potty," and yet being given clear permission to continue eliminating in his diaper.

A parent asks, "So what about training pants or pull-ups?"

Training pants and what are generically known as "pull-ups" are diapers in disguise. (The product name Pull-Ups is a registered trademark of Kimberly-Clark, but the term is now used generically in the same way that facial tissues, no matter the manufacturer, are known as "Kleenex.") As the reader will see in the next chapter, I recommend what Dr. Benjamin Spock endorsed in 1985: During toilet training, the child should wear no clothing below the waist (unless he or she is out in public). The sensation of bulky fabric being worn around the midsection is associated with permission to eliminate at will. Quite simply, if one wants to change a child's habit, *one must change as many of the cues that are supporting that habit as possible.* Pull-ups do nothing but substitute one feeling for another one that is almost identical. I am convinced that disposable-diaper manufacturers know the use of pull-ups makes toilet training more difficult and prolongs it indefinitely. These nefarious garments do not help either parent or child through the process. Quite the contrary; they hinder it.

NOT A MATTER OF LUCK: We began toilet training our little girl when she was nineteen months. It took no time at all. My friends were amazed, but refused to believe that early toilet training is generally possible. Instead, they told me I was lucky. In my opinion, it wasn't a matter of luck. Successful early training requires the parent to be the leader and to have a can-do attitude. I now have a newborn boy, and my friends are all saying that I won't be so lucky this time. I cannot wait to prove them wrong.

As time goes by, the window of opportunity (between eighteen and twenty-four months) opens and slowly shuts. After allowing this to happen, many new parents are dismayed and resentful when things do not work out the way they were told they would by readiness advocates. These parents are likely to become increasingly impatient and negative. In some cases, the child's toileting habits become such an obsession and source of anguish that the parent feels like a failure and the family becomes completely stressed out. Diane and I have witnessed this scenario many times, as many of these parents have turned to us for advice.

A HOPEFUL TESTIMONY! As a pediatrician and mother of four (who were all trained, boys and girls, before their second birthdays), I now discuss toilet training at the fifteen- or eighteen-month checkup. I discuss the window of opportunity that children display before the terrible twos begin and suggest that this age child wants to please his parents, which is less and less the case as he passes his second birthday. This advice flies in the face of what future pediatricians are taught during our residencies, but parents who listen and act on my advice are consistently amazed at how much easier it is to train a child under two than to wait.

Most concerning is that while the late-toilet-training trend has continued, researchers have noted an upsurge in toileting problems among children. Two examples:

- Pediatrician Bruce Taubman's research published in Pediatrics included a sample of 482 children. Taubman found that as the age at which training commenced increased, so did the likelihood of what he calls "stool toileting refusal" (child refuses to use the toilet for bowel movements). Half the children in his study who trained between three-and-one-half and four experienced this problem, as did nearly three out of four of the children who trained after their fourth birthdays.[9]

- In 2000, Belgian researchers reported a connection between problems of bladder control and "liberal" toilet-training methods.[10]

Other problems associated with late training include increased constipation, soiling, withholding, smearing, and bedwetting. If persistent, these conditions can lead to serious medical and behavioral problems, embarrassing social situations, invasive medical procedures, and enormous anxiety for the entire family. Children in this category may even qualify to attend Boston Children's Hospital's "Toilet School," a toilet-training day camp for children four and older who have not yet, as Brazelton puts it, "complied with toilet training pressure." In other words, these kids are not stubborn little despots who have seized on refusing to use the toilet as a means of controlling their families; they are rebels with a noble cause.

A PROUD MOM WRITES: My son was completely potty trained—nighttime, too—at twenty-three months! I have six friends who have children one year older than my son, and only two of those kids are trained. When I tell one of these moms of my son's experience, there is always shock. One mom told me to be sure that I am not the one who is trained instead of my child, and two moms warned me that early training could cause relapses that are hard to recover from. One mom said that she didn't even approach it until her son was two-and-one-half because she was told by her pediatrician that younger children just don't have the control or emotional maturity to master it, and she didn't want to harm the child's "self-esteem." By the way, all of these moms have at least one college degree, and some have two. The brainwashing that has occurred in this society to sell more disposable diapers runs deep!

T. BERRY BRAZELTON AND
CHILD-CENTERED TOILET TRAINING

In 1962, pediatrician T. Berry Brazelton kicked toilet-training controversies up a few notches with the publication of "A Child-Oriented Approach to Toilet Training" (*Pediatrics,* January 1962), a summary of what is properly called field research carried out in his Cambridge, Massachusetts, pediatric clinic between 1951 and 1961. In this influential article, Brazelton took the position that toilet training should be postponed until after the second birthday, his premise being that the pre-two child's nervous system was not sufficiently mature, and that a child's interest in bladder and bowel control would increase during his third year of life, as did his general desire for independence and mastery.

Brazelton claimed that 90 percent of 1,170 parents followed his recommendation to postpone toilet training. He made no distinction between bowel and bladder training, but reported that, on average, daytime training was completed at twenty-eight months and nighttime control at thirty-three. The crux of his study, and his selling point for postponing training until after the second birthday, was that fewer than 2 percent of the children studied showed evidence of soiling, constipation, or bedwetting at age five, the usual report at the time being between 10 and 20 percent.

From a strictly scientific point of view, Brazelton's study was highly flawed. First, he was obviously attempting to prove a point rather than simply trying to discover the truth. Second, he had no control group. Third, his data could not be independently verified. Fourth, because his data consisted solely of anecdotal reports, his study could not be replicated. For all these reasons, it is impossible to draw accurate conclusions or posit accurate generalizations from his study. Despite the flaws in his methods, he drew hard-and-fast conclusions and put forward equally hard-and-fast recommendations, which were readily accepted in mainstream pediatric and psychological circles and have had a far-reaching impact on modern child-rearing practice ever since.

Brazelton's article became the springboard for his ever-expanding notions about readiness. After it was published, pediatricians and psychologists began to think of learning to use the toilet as being no different from learning to walk in that they considered both a matter of maturation and the child's natural urge to achieve competence and master the environment. When a child's nervous system and muscle control had matured to a certain level, the child would walk. No one had to *teach* him to walk. He would walk *because he wanted to*. Likewise, Brazelton proposed that when a child's nervous system and muscle control had matured to a certain level, the child would begin controlling his bowels and bladder, and with minimal guidance would begin using the toilet. No one would have to *make* him use the toilet. He would use the toilet *because he wanted to*, just as he wanted to master other aspects of his environment. The problem with the analogy is that learning to walk is not essential to a child's successful integration into society.

In one stroke, Brazelton all but abolished the role of the parent as an authoritative teacher of toileting skills. Despite the glaring shortcomings of his study, his thesis gained almost instant acceptance in the professional community. In fact, Diane and I have been unable to find anyone at the time who dared disagree with Brazelton. This overnight change in belief is an example of what two researchers noted in a 1977 analysis of toilet-training trends: "Infant care writers [tend to change] opinions in unison, without the benefit of strong empirical evidence."[11]

Interestingly enough, careful analysis of Brazelton's data—his pure numbers as opposed to his very biased interpretation of those numbers—reveals that his study actually supports pre-two toilet training. Consider: Thirty-eight percent of parents in the study began training by eighteen months, and 90 percent had started by twenty-four months. As it turns out, more than half the children in Brazelton's study were successfully trained by twenty-four months, and that figure jumps to three out of four by twenty-seven months.

Obviously, Brazelton's own data support the notion that toilet training initiated before the second birthday is unlikely to be associated with later problems of bladder and bowel control. His data and his interpretations simply do not match. Why no one noticed this and raised the issue is a mystery. Perhaps Brazelton's affiliation with Harvard University was intimidating, as might have been the fact that his article was published in the most prestigious pediatric journal in the world. Perhaps pediatricians and psychologists were ready to embrace any new potty-training paradigm in order to appear progressive. In any event, Brazelton became America's resident potty pundit, and toilet training would never be the same.

2

TOILET-BABBLE

AUTHOR'S NOTE: *Because pediatrician T. Berry Brazelton has had such a profound effect on American toilet-training practice over the past fifty years, it is appropriate to allot a separate chapter—this one—to a review and critique of his toilet-training philosophy and advice. He and I are 180 degrees apart on this issue. However, whereas I think Dr. Brazelton's toilet-training advice caused much unnecessary difficulty for parents and children, I have no doubt but that he is a fine man who sincerely believes that his advice is in the best interests of all concerned.*

Forty-plus years have elapsed since pediatrician T. Berry Brazelton published his original findings. In the meantime, he has not conducted any research that would qualify as truly scientific (using a randomly selected control group and what is known as a double-blind research design) but has only collected anecdotal reports from parents, who tend not to be the most objective reporters when it comes to the behavior of their own children. Nonetheless, he claims to have conclusively identified toilet training's readiness signs, states that pre-two training—because that age child is rarely "ready"—is potentially harmful and requires excessive parental pressure, and assures parents that it is not at all problematic for intelligent human beings to continue soiling and wetting themselves until they are three or even four years old. Those are my words, not his; nonetheless, that is a fair characterization of his message.

FREUD REDUX

Over the years, Brazelton has become increasingly fond of using dramatic statements of pure conjecture to bolster his contentions. Two such examples from his 1974 book *Toddlers and Parents:*

- He asserts that children "value the bowel movement as part of themselves and worry about it going down the drain."

- After watching young children play with a large toilet display at a children's museum, he concludes that children need to work through a certain amount of anxiety over using the toilet.

Around the beginning of the millennium, I coined the term *toilet-babble* to describe statements of this whimsical sort. Brazelton's writings on toilet training are replete with similar flights of fancy.

Concerning the first example just given, one must puzzle at how he came to know that toddlers attach "value" to their bowel movements and experience anxiety at seeing them flushed away. Young children simply do not say things like, "You know, I worry a lot about what happens to my poop, which I am rather fond of, when it goes down the potty." Bottom line: Brazelton's contention is far-fetched.

Brazelton's not alone in this belief, however. On his Web site, pediatrician and author William Sears claims that many children "are afraid of seeing parts of themselves come out of their body and go swoosh down the drain."[12] Really? I am unaware of any objective evidence that supports this imaginative contention.

Trying to prove the point, apparently, Brazelton goes on to say that toddlers become worried about where bathtub water goes when it drains out of the tub, and then he further stretches credulity by asserting that toddlers worry "whether they might get sucked down too." Excuse me? I've worked with parents and children for forty years. I've helped raise two children to whom I gave numerous baths when they were toddlers. Never have I witnessed or heard a parent report anxiety on the part of a child at seeing water drain out of the tub. My kids thought it was entertaining, and wanted to remain in the tub until all the water was gone. That is the norm, not children jumping up and beginning to scream when the drain is activated. Because anything is possible, I'll grant that some child, somewhere, has developed this fear, but to suggest that it is common is indefensible. Brazelton even claims that some children may worry about something coming back up the bathtub drain or the toilet bowl. It begins to sound like he's been watching too many bad horror movies.

Concerning the idea that kids playing with an oversize toilet are trying to work through related psychological anxieties, let me assure the reader that children taking such delight is no more psychologically significant than children liking to play with toy kitchens. It certainly cannot be concluded that when children play in toy kitchens they are actually trying to work through "food-preparation anxiety."

Reading Brazelton's writings on the subject of toilet training, it becomes obvious that he's been greatly influenced by Freudian theory. That's understandable, given that he did postgraduate study in child psychiatry at Massachusetts General Hospital in the 1950s, when Freud's influence in academia—and especially in Ivy League territory—was at its peak. In fact, it often sounds like he's channeling Freud. And like Freud's, Brazelton's speculations on the inner workings of the human psyche are highly imaginative.

Take his theory on the effect of flushing on the young child's psyche. In actual fact, toddlers are generally awestruck by flushing and will want to do it over and over again. That's why they are likely, when their parents aren't looking, to put all manner of objects down the toilet and try to flush them away. Toddlers are a plumber's best friend. For the typical toddler, flushing is not anxiety arousing. It's sport!

Toddlers are also fascinated with the play possibilities inherent in poop, as they are the play possibilities of everything else. That's why, if left to their own devices, many of them discover the joys of finger-painting with poop. The desire to explore and experiment is the dominant characteristic of toddlerhood, not anxiousness over where things go.

Brazelton extends his fantastical speculations to the matter of diaper changing, proposing that when a child gives up diapers he gives up a certain amount of intimacy that parents must make up for in other ways. He asks, "Why would a two-year-old want to give up these close times for a cold potty?" By raising the notion that toilet training disrupts the parent–child bond, Brazelton again raises the anxiety-arousing specter of potentially devastating psychological harm. His book really should be titled *How to Make Toilet Training the Most Nerve-Wracking Experience of Your Life*. In fact, largely because of this sort of fantastical toilet-babble, toilet training for many mothers has become stressful, anxiety arousing, frustrating, and guilt ridden. For some, it proves to be the most stressful experience of their entire motherhoods. And no wonder. After all, Brazelton basically tells parents that in order to toilet train properly, they must become quasi therapists to their children so as to prevent, or at least minimize, the psychological trauma inherent in the process.

I am reminded of an anecdote once related to me by a journalist who was writing a piece on toilet training that contrasted my views with Brazelton's. She told me that she was unable to get to the man himself but interviewed one of his staff, who told her that pre-two toilet training, when initiated by the parent, "robs a child of autonomy." That's a prime example of toilet-babble. It is unfounded, impossible to verify, and wholly speculative. It's the sort of warning that causes parents to believe that if they make one misstep in toilet training, they will cause their child great psychological harm. This sort of warning has the effect of instilling anxiety into parents and causing them to delay toilet training well past the time when it would have gone smoothly.

In all fairness, Brazelton does constantly emphasize what is undeniably true: Ultimately, the *child* will decide whether and when he uses the toilet. Pressuring a child to use the toilet will almost surely backfire. Brazelton makes his mistake in equating *any* initiative on a parent's part with pressure. The fact is, toilet training will almost surely have to be initiated by the parent because, even when the window of opportunity is most open—between eighteen and twenty-four months—only the rare child is going to initiate the process himself, much less self-train.

A PROUD MOM REPORTS: I am the mother of four, all of whom have been trained by their second birthdays. They would sit on the potty and play with a toy or look at a book. They gradually got the hang of it to where they would tell me when they had to go. It was a completely natural process with no grief for any of us.

Let's face it: Toilet training, like teaching any other social skill, including table manners and proper greetings, is a parental responsibility. I've never heard of a child developing proper table manners on his own, without parental correction and teaching. And make no mistake about it: Learning to dispose of one's own body wastes discreetly and properly is a social skill that is necessary to civilizing a human being. It is one of many learned behaviors that distinguishes us from animals and enables us to live cooperatively in organized social groups. The child who does not master this skill is going to offend people, just as he would if he sat at someone's table and ate like a jungle beast. Furthermore, the earlier a child benefits from this civilizing influence, the better, for him and everyone around him.

READINESS, SCHMEDINESS

In his 1992 book, *Touchpoints*—exactly thirty years after reporting that a supermajority of the children in his 1962 study were learning to use the toilet by twenty-four months of age—Brazelton shrugs off any toileting interest on the part of pre–two-year-olds. To a mother who comments how her toddler is aware of his bowel movements and pulls at his diaper, Brazelton responds that this means only that "when the time comes, he will want to be in control of his own toilet habits." It is more likely to mean that he finds a messy diaper uncomfortable. I would tell this mother that the time has come to help her child learn what he is obviously capable of learning and will *want* to learn as soon as he realizes the pleasures of dry, clean underwear. That Brazelton actually discouraged this mother from toilet training a child who is capable of mastering the task is just plain wrong. Unfortunately, it seems characteristic.

Several years ago, I received an e-mail from the mother of a child who had shown desire to use the toilet before twelve months and had mastered the process in no time. The mother reported that she had called Brazelton to ask whether he'd ever heard of this in a child so young. According to her, Brazelton became upset, and accused her of "forcing" her infant to use the toilet, implying that she had already done the child great harm. Keep in mind that up until the 1940s many children in America were using the toilet successfully before their first birthdays, and there is no evidence that such early toilet training caused psychological harm to these kids. To this mother's credit, she stood her ground, and told Brazelton she really wasn't interested in his editorial comments; she only wanted to know whether he'd heard of this before. For him to deny the obvious—that the child in question was obviously ready to use the toilet before she turned one, and that toilet training the child had been a cakewalk—says that Brazelton doesn't want to hear anything that might contradict his personal belief system.

In *Touchpoints,* Brazelton asserts that the following five signs of supposed readiness should be present in a child's behavior before parents start toilet training:

- The child is over the excitement of walking and likes to sit down.

- Understands simple distinctions, as in the difference between the parents' toilet and his potty.

- Likes to imitate others, especially his parents.

- Possesses an appreciation for orderliness (e.g., he puts things in their proper places), "which can be transferred to urine and bowel movements."

- Isn't negative when given instructions.

Spock's 1968 list of readiness signs and Brazelton's 1992 list are similar in that both lists emanated not from research but from Spock's and Brazelton's creative imaginations. The crucial difference is that whereas Spock intended his list to serve as simply a general guide and encouraged parents to begin training by eighteen months irrespective of signs, Brazelton warned parents against starting training until readiness behaviors have emerged.

Brazelton's indicators serve the purpose of creating the impression that he's delved deeply into the mysteries of toilet training, more deeply than anyone before him. They put a pseudoscientific aura around a process that is not at all complex and hardly scientific. Also significant and highly ironic is the fact that Brazelton's five readiness signs are present in many an eighteen-month-old child! Yet he would apparently argue that a child that age who exhibits all five readiness signs is not old enough to be toilet trained.

Keep in mind that in the mid-1950s, when researchers from several major universities found that 80 percent of American children were successfully trained by age twenty-four months, close to 100 percent of America's parents paid no heed to readiness signs, and there's no evidence that this widespread ignorance resulted in any harm to children. Taking myself as an example, I was trained in 1949, right around my second birthday. That was within the norm back then. My mother made an arbitrary decision to start my training, and she told me it lasted less than a week. Perhaps I'm in a deep state of denial, but I don't believe I am burdened with unresolved issues relating to my bladder and bowel functions. Furthermore, I have yet to encounter a member of my generation who has admitted to having or seemed to have debilitating psychological blockages when it comes to eliminating body waste or being in the presence of white porcelain objects.

After providing a useless, if not confounding, set of supposed readiness criteria, Brazelton describes the steps necessary to successful toilet training, always reminding parents that they should allow a child to refuse to use the toilet and should immediately put a child back in diapers after an accident so as not to make him "feel like a failure." How he knows that a toddler who has just had an accident and whose parents stay the course (do not return him to diapers) will feel like a failure is yet another mystery. In fact, it seems to me that putting a child back in diapers after an accident is a clear message that he failed. In any case, this is nothing more than an example of Brazelton's habit of making unsupportable claims that have the effect of mystifying what is an uncomplicated process, thus increasing the potential for parent anxiety. Concerning diapers and accidents, I contend (consistent with Spock) that once the decision is made to toilet train a child, nothing short of a major illness necessitating the child's hospitalization or some other prolonged emergency (more than a brief crisis, in other words) is sufficient cause to call off the training. Nothing will kill the success of toilet training more than starting, then stopping and returning the child to diapers, then waiting, then starting, then stopping, and so on.

On the matter of accidents, most experts advise that when a child in training has one, the parents should reassure him that it's okay. Rubbish! It's *not* okay, and the child should most definitely *not* hear a message that contradicts what his parents are expecting him to do. There's a way of doing that without telling the child he's a miserable failure: "You wee-weed on yourself. When you feel a poop/wee-wee coming, you must sit down on your potty, like I showed you, and put your poop/wee-wee in there. I know you can do it, and you'll do better next time." A message of that sort gives accurate feedback, reinforces the goal, and sends an empowering message to the child: "I know you can do this."

Brazelton would probably disapprove, and even some readers might be taken slightly aback at the tone of that very straightforward statement. Some might even feel that it's a bit negative. The fact is, the statement is truthful, and, believe it or not, even very young children can tolerate the truth, plainly and noncritically spoken. The child has just made a mistake. In order for him to improve his performance, to eventually master this new task, it is vital that he receive accurate feedback and clear, supportive instructions from his parents. It's one thing to calmly say, "You had an accident. You didn't do what I told you to do." It's quite another to yell, "You're a miserable brat!" at the top of your lungs. In short, it is possible to tell a child that he's made a mistake without making him feel worthless.

At the core of Brazelton's toilet-training approach is the belief that using the toilet is just too much to ask of a pre–two-year-old. He tirelessly reiterates that the requirements of toilet training result in enormous and sometimes incapacitating pressures on children. He seems to regret that we have to expect this of them at all. According to Brazelton, any refusal, show of anxiety, hesitation, or unusual behavior on the part of the child occurs because toilet training involves so much psychological stress. In recognition of the harm that this enormously demanding and potentially traumatic process can force on a child, parents should immediately back off and revert to diapers if the child has an accident. He says, "Repeated failures are likely to occur because [the child is] just not ready. Diapers need to be used . . . as a way of relieving her from the fear of making mistakes." Hear me clearly: This is very bad advice.

27

However—and bear with me here—there have been times when I've told a mother to stop training and return her child to diapers. But I've given this advice not because the child was not ready but because the *mother* was not ready. She was highly anxious, micromanaging, and thereby creating a huge resistance problem. Under those circumstances, a mother needs to back off, take a deep breath, relax, and give herself some time before she begins training again. In other words, I give that advice when the mental state of the *mother,* not the child, is the issue.

Remember, *accidents are inevitable.* Parents who follow Brazelton's advice to the proverbial T will wind up starting and stopping the process numerous times, thus giving the child no clear and consistent message as to their expectations. *That's* confusing.

In the final analysis, and for all his claims of respecting children, Brazelton seems to seriously underestimate their capabilities. And for all his claims of wanting to do nothing more than make parenting easier and more enjoyable, Brazelton causes parents to question the legitimacy of their own authority.

In *Toilet Training the Brazelton Way* (2004), Brazelton recognizes what he calls a "recurrent surge of delays in successful toilet training." In other words, he acknowledges that toilet-training problems—the most prevalent being withholding bowel movements (self-constipation) and stubborn refusal to use the toilet—are on the increase, as they have been for some time, and that on average children are being trained later and later. He blames these problematic trends on day care centers that pressure parents to train children prematurely. I believe that the increase in toilet-training problems is due to parents training later, not earlier, and parents using a toilet-training method—one Brazelton himself all but crafted—that is dysfunctional.

SAME OLD, SAME OLD

By 2004, Brazelton has expanded his five readiness signs to seven:

- The child is not as excited about walking and being on her feet all the time.

- Possesses receptive language.

- Can say "No!"

- Has started putting things where they belong.

- Imitates the parents' behavior.

- Urinates and defecates at predictable times.

- Is aware of her body.

Again, there is simply no good reason to believe that any one of these must be present before parents can initiate successful toilet training. Again, Brazelton cloaks what is essentially a contrivance in the guise of science. And again, most of the behaviors in question, in most children, emerge before age two. In some children, for example, receptive language emerges before the first birthday, and in most children it is solidly established by eighteen months. In fact, I cannot identify one of these seven signs that is not likely to emerge before age two. Yet Brazelton makes it clear: Toilet training is not appropriate for the typical pre–two-year-old, and parents should wait for all seven signs to appear before starting the process. He then says, "Later on, there will be more advanced signs that a child is ready."

What's this? Brazelton seems to be saying that even if all seven readiness behaviors emerge before age two—which, remember, is highly likely—the parent should still not go ahead with toilet training. Instead, the parent should wait for even more signs. Again, he seems determined, at the cost of simplicity and clarity, to admit that his own standards permit pre-two toilet training. He's staked out a position, and he is going to defend it against the facts, no matter what.

Before enumerating his "advanced" indicators of readiness, however, Brazelton indulges in more toilet-babble. A two-year-old, he says, has developed a sense of what child development specialists call "object permanence." This is the ability to understand that objects continue to exist even when they are removed from sight. This ability is prerequisite, says Brazelton, to the child being "ready to say goodbye to poop." No kidding.

Statements of this sort cause me to question whether Brazelton is as well versed in the field of child development as he is generally regarded. In the first place, it has long been known in child development circles that object permanence, first identified by Swiss psychologist Jean Piaget, is fairly well established by eight or nine months of age. (In recent years, however, several researchers have challenged that, saying it is established even earlier.)

In the second place, although I happen to think that it's great and foolish fun for parent and child to stand over the toilet while the flush is swirling and say "Bye-bye, poop!" I think it's downright silly to imply that this is somehow essential to the child's mental health, that it helps him deal with potentially overpowering feelings of loss and separation.

A HAPPY MOTHER REPORTS: When my twin boys were finished toilet training at twenty-six months, their very pleased pediatrician and I had a discussion in which he told me that when he began practicing it was assumed that children would be trained by or around their second birthdays. If a child wasn't trained by then, pediatricians began looking for physical reasons why the child was not able to control his bodily functions. When I asked him why he thought things had changed so dramatically, he said, "Brazelton and disposable diapers." He also said that it was his opinion that it is psychologically damaging to a child to not have control of his bowel and bladder when he was clearly able to control them.

As is the case with all of Brazelton's criteria and pronouncements on the matter of readiness signs, his second set of supposedly "more advanced" readiness markers is not based on true research. It is based primarily on his rigid belief that what almost all children younger than two years old around the world accomplished before the 1960s, they are not capable of accomplishing today; or if they are capable, it is only at great psychological cost. Here is Brazelton's list of advanced indicators:

- What he calls "toilet talk." For example, the child announces with pride, "I went poop, Mommy!"
- Playfully pretending to use the potty.
- The ability to dress and undress himself.
- An awareness of how other people use the potty.
- Increased imitation.

Brazelton maintains that these advanced signs don't emerge until approximately the second birthday. In fact, the first two—"toilet talk" and pretending to use the potty—are usually evident before age two. On the other hand, most children are not able to dress and undress themselves until age three. In all likelihood, most kids will express awareness of how other people use the toilet before age two. I know mine did.

Brazelton says that imitation becomes "more exciting and complex" shortly after a child turns two, and that two-year-olds imitate one another during play. Neither of these statements is consistent with established developmental knowledge.

First, imitation of adults, especially parents, is in part an indicator of a child's willingness to cooperate with those same adults. That does not describe two-year-olds. Twos have a reputation for being "terrible" for good reasons. Imitation usually peaks during the *fourth* year of life (between the third and fourth birthdays), not the third.

Second, two-year-olds most definitely do *not* tend to imitate one another during play. Even in a group setting, the typical two-year-old child's play is solitary. He doesn't pay much attention to what other kids are doing until he notices what one of them is playing with, at which point he's likely to try and snatch it. In a group setting, two-year-olds are like separate island nations that launch occasional preemptive strikes at one another.

Brazelton further claims that toilet training will be easier after the second birthday because two-year-olds want to please their parents. That certainly does not describe most of the twos I've known or encountered vicariously through parental description. Most of those toddlers have been "terrible" to one vexing degree or another. The typical toddler does not want to please; rather, he wants to be pleased. He does not want to obey; he wants to be obeyed. One begins to wonder whether Brazelton really and truly knows children or only has preconceived ideas about them.

In his 2004 book, Brazelton cites women of other cultures who train their children in infancy. He admits to being impressed by these children's capability and their parents' relaxed attitude. He then does a flip-flop, proposing that "in our mainstream hygienic culture, we must find other ways to respect the child's role." He claims that training an American child before eighteen months (the norm in undeveloped countries) must of necessity be "forced, rigid, punitive and without the child's active participation." Without realizing that he's doing so, Brazelton identifies the key to successful training no matter the child's age: a relaxed attitude on the part of the mother (or primary trainer).

It appears that Brazelton is trying desperately to reconcile the facts, including that children in other cultures are trained early with no apparent harm (as was once the case in America), with his rigid belief that early training is harmful. The attempt is desperate because there is no possibility of reconciliation here. Either Brazelton is wrong or the facts are wrong; and facts, by definition, are not wrong.

YET ANOTHER COMMON-SENSIBLE MOM: I started training my son at fourteen months of age. Within a couple of weeks he could tell me he had to go by saying, "Uh-oh." He is twenty-two months old, now, and doesn't wear diapers at all, not even at night. My friends, meanwhile, have been told by their pediatricians not to train their three-year-olds because they aren't ready. My son is proof that early potty training is possible if the parent recognizes the child's interest and is willing to go against the grain.

Readiness propaganda is prevalent in both modern parenting resources and the mainstream media. Take parenting pundit Elizabeth Pantley, for example. In *The No-Cry Potty Training Solution*, published in 2006, Pantley recommends that potty training take place during the "magical age span" of two-and-one-half to four.[13] Remember that research has determined that the risk of problems increases significantly after Pantley's recommended—"magical" even—start time of two-and-one-half years. In her book, she approaches training from what she calls the "more common toddler-readiness approach."

Indeed, the pseudoscientific readiness approach is the more common approach these days, but (to cite but one example of many) it's also become common for today's parents to allow pacifiers well past the second birthday, long past the time experts advise getting rid of them. In other words, the fact that a parenting practice is common is no recommendation. But given the fact that the professional community has rallied around the notion of toilet readiness, it's no wonder that it has captivated so many American parents, who now tend to be skeptical of any notions that run counter to it. As a result, whereas *early* in toilet training once meant twelve to eighteen months, its popular meaning now is that thirty months (two-and-one-half) is the earliest a child is going to be ready, with most children being ready around age three, but that it is not a problem if a child shows lack of readiness until age four or even older, hence the advent of what I call "Little Depends": disposable diapers that fit children up to 50 pounds and 42 inches tall, which are averages for children ages four through six.

To the disgrace of the profession, many pediatricians have a blanket policy of discouraging parents from beginning to train before age three. These pediatricians often assure parents that their children will train themselves without much assistance sometime between ages three and four. This wrongheaded advice has caused parents tremendous grief, especially when they find themselves dealing with a four-year-old who not only shows no interest in using the toilet but absolutely refuses to sit on it, no matter what enticements his parents present. What parents hear from people who present themselves as toilet-training experts, their pediatricians, and the media is further reinforced in many a parent peer group, where it becomes heretical for a mother to violate the peer group's implied understanding that no child of any mother in the group will be trained before age three.

I have heard numerous testimonies from mothers who suddenly became persona non grata among their friends simply because they dared violate this norm and toilet train their children "early."

If a parenting resource even mentions the possibility of pre-two toilet training, it will almost surely be to warn off any parent who may be considering it, conjuring up visions of psychological catastrophe. Parents who have no reason to believe that "experts" might not know what they're talking about then become fearful of pre-two training even if confronted with a pre–two-year-old who is obviously interested in using the potty. Even parents who possess little toilet-training anxiety have been led to believe that if they wait until their children are at least three before toilet training, it will be a breeze. So they wait, and the convenience of disposable diapers means that the parents pay no significant price (other than the unnecessary cost of the disposables themselves) during the waiting. They pay a heavy emotional price later, when they decide they've waited long enough and then try to persuade their kids to at least give sitting on the toilet a try or something equally limp-wristed. But who can blame them? The typical parent has no way of knowing that the concept of readiness was invented, cut from whole cloth. The average parent has no way of knowing that not one of the following claims is supported by credible scientific evidence:

- Certain specific developmental milestones must be cleared before successful toilet training can begin (historical evidence does not support this).

- The older the child, the easier toilet training will be (exactly the opposite is true, as we will see).

- Toilet training a child before supposed readiness behaviors emerge will harm the child's psychological development (unsupported by any objectively gathered evidence).

"But what about self-training?" a reader asks. "If a parent does wait, will the child eventually train himself?"

I've heard very few stories of children who, on their own and without even the subtlest hints from their parents, have spontaneously signaled that they want to use the potty and used it without incident from that point. They roughly equal the number of children brought to my attention who have learned to read on their own before going to school. And the parallel doesn't end there, because like the child who teaches himself to read before going to school, almost every story of self–toilet training has involved *a child who was not yet two years old.* In fact, the method I will present in Chapter 3 is at heart a self-training model. I am convinced, as you will see, that the less involved parents are in the process, the more quickly children will master the skill. In the context of my very old-fashioned model, the parent is a consultant who merely sets the stage properly, communicates properly, and responds to mistakes properly. I trust that the child does indeed want mastery, but unlike Brazelton, I am convinced that the optimal time to introduce this opportunity for mastery to the child is before age two.

IN CONCLUSION

Brazelton simply does not acknowledge—one might go so far as to say he denies—the importance of the parent's role in toilet training. His advice is child-centric to a fault. He believes that the child's feelings should dominate any other consideration. So, for example, if the child balks at using the toilet, the parent should put diapers back on the child. If the child has an accident, the parent should put diapers back on the child. If the child displays any anxiety over sitting on the toilet and releasing, the parent should back off and put diapers back on the child. Following his advice cannot possibly result in an effortless, enjoyable toilet-training process.

Brazelton's advice arises from his belief that toilet training is fraught with apocalyptic psychological consequences. By communicating this belief to parents, he causes parents to dread having to toilet train, to approach training with trepidation and anxiety, and to send their children mixed messages about exactly what is expected. A child who senses that his parents are not sure of themselves—and young children sense this almost immediately—will respond by resisting the parents' tense efforts to move him toward sitting and releasing on the toilet.

Like any other teaching, toilet training requires a show of calm, purposeful authority, an authority that communicates to the child exactly what he is and is not to do, and is not afraid to speak correctively to the child when such correction is called for. For a child to become convinced that he can master using the toilet, his parents must have complete confidence in his ability to master using the toilet. Brazelton's advice, I contend, weakens parental confidence, weakens parental resolve, and sets the stage for unnecessary toilet-training hassles.

Please don't misunderstand me on this point: I am not saying that parents should try to control a child's toileting habits, because the only person who can (and should) control those habits is the child, and the parent's proper role is to help the child establish that control. I am saying that toilet training requires leadership and a clear demonstration of positive authority (a demonstration that communicates confidence to the child). Brazelton's advice is not consistent with that objective. The problem with Brazelton's advice is not just that he advocates waiting long past the window of maximum opportunity has opened and shut but that he undermines the authority and confidence parents must carry into the process in order for it to go smoothly. In other words, even if Brazelton believed, as I do, that the time to toilet train is between eighteen and twenty-four months, parents who followed his advice would still have problems because his advice fails to affirm and strengthen a proper parental attitude.

For example, and by contrast, I believe that if a child shows resistance, the parent should stay the course. I believe that if a child has an accident, which is inevitable, the parent should stay the course. I even believe that if the child shows fear, the parent should stay the course. I believe parents know what is best for children. I believe parents should empathize with the irrational fears that children sometimes manifest, but I also believe that parents should not let a child's irrational fears define the course of the child's upbringing or any aspect of it.

Furthermore, thirty years of experience in consulting with thousands of parents about toilet-training matters has yielded too much positive feedback for me to believe anything other than that I am right about this. That is not arrogance. That is confidence. I have confidence that my advice works. Likewise, I want parents to be confident of themselves as leaders of children where toilet training is concerned, and I want confident parents to create children who are confident that they are capable of mastering this simple process.

CHAPTER BIBLIOGRAPHY

References to Dr. Brazelton's toilet-training advice came from the following of his books:

- *What Every Baby Knows*. Addison-Wesley, 1987.

- *Touchpoints: Your Child's Emotional and Behavioral Development.* Addison-Wesley, 1992.

- *Toilet Training the Brazelton Way* (with Dr. Joshua Sparrow). DaCapo Press, 2004.

- *Touchpoints Three to Six* (with Dr. Joshua Sparrow). Perseus Publishing, 2001.

3

THE SIMPLE JOYS OF
"NAKED AND $75"

Before beginning a description of "my" toilet-training method (the quotation marks denote that I have no right to ownership, as the method is the norm in many traditional cultures), which I call "Naked and $75," I should warn you that Dr. T. Berry Brazelton once told an interviewer that said method is "very logical—for a puppy."[14]

That seems like a logical place to begin, which I'm going to do by asking the reader one simple question: Given that a puppy can be successfully and quickly house trained at three to six months of age, what sense does it make to think that a human being cannot be successfully toilet trained until he is at least two years of age and in most cases much older?

Apparently, I have more faith in and respect for the intelligence of eighteen- to twenty-four-month-old human beings than do some intellectuals. I believe it insults a child's intelligence to let him urinate and defecate on himself well past his second birthday. Allowing him to soil himself in this uncivilized manner is the worst sort of disrespect.

I will now ask a second, multiple-choice question, again having to do with puppies, since that seems to be a point of contention: Is it easier to house train a four-month-old puppy or a one-year-old dog?

It is easier to train the four-month-old puppy! Furthermore, it is easier *by far*. Anyone who possesses a fair understanding of dogs can house train a four-month-old puppy in several days to a week. If you wait until a dog is a year old before starting training, you'll find that the devil must be paid first. The four-month-old puppy gets it very quickly; the one-year-old dog has a very difficult time getting it. You take him for an hour-long walk, during which he sniffs every vertical object in sight but produces no prize. Finally, exasperated, you take him home. Less than a minute after you bring him through the door, a certain smell assaults your olfactory organ. This sort of thing goes on for three to six months before, finally, success! Even then, you're likely to have to deal with the occasional accident for years to come.

But why? After all, the one-year-old dog is more familiar with his handler's signals, has outgrown a good deal of his hyperactive puppyness, and is more easily trainable when it comes to other things, such as walking cooperatively next to his handler. The resolution of this paradox has to do with the fact that house training is not primarily a matter of the dog's level of experience; rather, it is primarily a matter of habit, and the longer one allows the puppy to eliminate at will, wherever and whenever the urge strikes, the stronger the habit will become. The harder it will be, therefore, to teach the older dog the new "trick."

Likewise, the longer parents allow a child to eliminate at will, wherever and whenever the urge strikes, the stronger the "eliminate whenever I want to" habit will become, and the harder it will be to teach the older child to pay attention to certain physical signals emanating from his lower regions and to control the bodily processes associated with them.

So I thank Dr. Brazelton for his unintentional inspiration. Indeed, there are several illustrative parallels between house training a dog and toilet training a child:

First, neither the dog nor the child needs to be punished in order to learn bowel and bladder control. In both cases, punishment is a function of frustration on the part of the handler or parent, and in both cases, punishment will set the process back.

Second, in both cases, the keys to success are clear direction and encouragement. Shown the alternative, a puppy will quickly realize that eliminating outside the boundaries of one's living space is preferable to eliminating inside those boundaries ("fouling one's own nest"). Show the alternative, encourage the puppy's success, and the puppy will quickly realize the benefits of being house trained. Likewise, show a child the alternative to sloppy, smelly diapers, encourage the child's success, and the child will quickly realize the benefits to himself of using the toilet. And believe me when I say it must be clear to the child that the benefit of using the toilet accrues primarily to him before he will begin using the toilet voluntarily and successfully. He will not cooperate as readily if the parent is acting as if this business of toilet training is for her benefit, that it's something she wants for herself, and desperately so.

The final parallels are perhaps the most important: In both house training a puppy and toilet training a child, one must (a) set the stage properly, (b) communicate expectations clearly, and (c) respond to mistakes appropriately. That's it! Does that sound complicated? No, of course it doesn't, and it isn't. In fact, it's simple, as you will see shortly.

But before sharing the simplicity and common sense of "Naked and $75" (N75) with you, let me sell it to you by enumerating its advantages over a readiness-based approach such as Brazelton's:

- N75 respects a child's intelligence and abilities.

- Parents gain early independence along with the child—independence from diaper changing and the expense of disposables and their accessories (powder, antirash ointment, and so on).

- N75 respects and affirms the importance of parental authority and leadership.

- The child who experiences the early benefits of N75 is unlikely to develop the various problems associated with later training, including withholding, constipation (and enlargement of the colon), and downright refusal to use the toilet.

- N75 is nonpsychological. It liberates parents from the anxiety of thinking that one misstep in toilet training will scar the child's delicate psyche for life, thus enabling a calm, controlled approach to helping the child gain control.

- N75 is nonintellectual in that parents are not required to consult laundry lists of readiness signs or made to believe they have to understand the supposedly complex psychology of the child in order to properly and successfully train.

- Children trained with N75 are happier kids, because they have mastered bowel and bladder control early.

- Because training after the second birthday is much more likely to lead to power struggles than pre-two N75, parents who use N75 are going to have a happier parenting experience.

To further inspire you, listen to a mom who has used N75 successfully with two children:

Q *I began "Naked and $75" when my second child, a daughter, was eighteen months and one week old. Initially, the accidents well outnumbered the successes, but I pushed on, and slowly but surely, things got better. It took about four weeks, but one day she just got it! She was nineteen months and five days old! That was ten days ago. This morning, we went shopping and she had her first success on a public toilet! Needless to say, I'm thrilled! I didn't begin toilet training my first until she was twenty-seven months old. I also used "Naked and $75" with her, and it was fairly easy, but this was even easier!*

A Note that this mom had greater success when she started training even earlier than she had with her first child—at eighteen months! And I dare say, not only did Mom have greater success, but her child had greater success as well. Cleanliness is a wonderful feeling.

THE PRELIMINARIES

TIMING: The book of Ecclesiastes tells us, "There's a time for everything and a season to every purpose under heaven."[15] Indeed, just as there are seasons to the growing of crops and the breeding of animals, there are seasons to the raising of a child. For example, the season for the discipline and socialization of a child, the time during which the child's character forms, lies during the ten years between the third and thirteenth birthdays—what I call the "Decade of Discipline." As most parents will attest, the attempt to discipline a child younger than three is a hit-or-miss proposition. On the other hand, discipline that has not been accomplished by the time a child is thirteen will be difficult to accomplish past that point.

And so it is with toilet training. Historical and cross-cultural data confirm beyond reasonable doubt that the peak season for toilet training is between eighteen and twenty-four months of age. However, this is not to say that children younger than eighteen months cannot be trained, because history tells us otherwise. One hundred years ago, most children were using the toilet independently by eighteen months. Even today, a good number of parents testify to having successfully trained children as young as twelve months. There's no doubt about it, children younger than eighteen months are able to develop the requisite awareness, communication skills, and bladder and bowel control. Nonetheless, I'm generally in favor of holding off until eighteen months. I believe—and this is confirmed by a good amount of personal and professional experience and parent testimony—that the supervision and assistance needed to train a child younger than eighteen months involves a cost to the parent that outweighs the benefits. Whereas it may take four months to completely train a fifteen-month-old, that same child at eighteen months of age can probably be trained in four weeks; in both cases, training is completed at nineteen months.

The occasional parent reports that her child showed interest in using the toilet well before eighteen months, and that the child essentially trained herself with minimal parental support. That's a horse of a different color, the distinguishing variable being that the child initiated the learning process, not the parent. This is akin to a child who, at age four, expresses interest in learning to read. As a general rule, I do not recommend formal reading instruction before age five or six, but I have no problem with parents encouraging and facilitating a younger child's obvious interest and motivation. Again, this boils down to the answer to one question: Who initiated the learning?

In the event your child initiates the toilet-training process before she is eighteen months of age, by all means provide whatever support she needs to attain mastery, but restrain your enthusiasm lest you begin inadvertently hovering and micromanaging. Give your child the space she needs to feel that *she* is directing her learning, not you. In this event, the recommendations I put forth in this chapter apply without significant revision, the sole exception being the obvious axiom: The younger the child, the more help the child is going to need with such things as sitting, pulling down underpants, wiping, and emptying her potty bowl in the "big potty."

If your child at, say, fourteen months initiates the process and then, after a period of progress, suddenly loses interest, you would do best to just let it be until she's at least eighteen months of age. An impatient effort to rekindle her interest may quickly evolve into a power struggle.

I have much stronger feelings about waiting past twenty-four months than I do about training before eighteen months. In the first place, children older than twenty-four months are more likely to have developed the knee-jerk defiance characteristic of the so-called terrible twos. The eighteen-month-old Dr. Jekyll who delights in doing what his parents tell him to do is very likely to be a twenty-six-month-old Mr. Hyde who delights in doing the exact opposite of what his parents tell him to do. Add to this the fact that the habit of eliminating without consideration of time or place is much, much stronger in a twenty-six-month-old than in an eighteen-month-old. Studies done by folks who have no stake in the outcome of the research have found that the risk of all manner of toilet-training problems, including flat-out refusal, increases the longer parents wait past a child's second birthday to train.

PROPER PREPARATION (IN PRAISE OF MINIMALISM): As your child approaches eighteen months, decide when to best fit this important project into your schedule and lifestyle, remembering that the earlier, the better. Mind you, the question is not *whether* it will fit into your schedule but *when* and *how* to best fit it in. In making this decision, keep in mind that you are going to have to make a full commitment for anywhere from two to six weeks, sometimes longer (at six weeks, however, if the light at the end of the tunnel is still not in sight, it's definitely time to up the ante, as described in the next chapter).

Once the decision's been made, a certain amount of preparation is absolutely necessary, but preparations can easily be overdone. An extensive, leave-no-stone-unturned approach will only build suspense about what will surely become, in your mind, the single most momentous day of your parenting life and maybe even your whole life. When that earthshaking day finally arrives, you will be brimming with anxiety and unable therefore to relax and (as Ringo put it so well) act naturally. Keep in mind that before the professional toilet-babblers made toilet training out to be complicated, detail-ridden, and fraught with psychological pitfalls, a mother's preparations consisted solely of purchasing a child's potty or a child-size potty seat that could be attached to the big toilet. At that point, she jumped into toilet training with both feet, which is exactly what Diane did with her second child: "I began training my second daughter at seventeen months on a whim, and it all worked out great! I had not prepared her, but I was willing to teach her, and was committed to not turning back. My attitude, I realize, made all the difference. I was not *trying* to toilet train her; I simply *was* toilet training her, and I dealt with problems as they arose instead of trying to anticipate everything that could go wrong. She was completely dry both night and day before twenty-four months!"

Seven months may seem like a long time, but Diane's daughter was daytime trained in less than two months, at nineteen months of age. Five months later, she was dry at night. (Although there is no definitive research on the subject, early toilet training seems to be associated with early night dryness.)

A POTTY OR A POTTY SEAT? Obviously, you're going to need to obtain a child-size potty or padded potty seat. I recommend the former, because potties facilitate a toddler's need for self-sufficiency, involve fewer safety concerns, are portable, and allow a parent to readily determine how much of which substance the child produced. I recommend that you purchase two or three (the same brand and color, preferably, and make it simple—no silly musical potties, please), one for each area of the house where your child spends significant time during the day (e.g., playroom, bedroom, and family den). You might even consider buying one for your car, especially if it has a flat back platform. I'm not suggesting that you lug a potty around with you as you shop, but until your child is fully trained it will be to his advantage as well as yours to have a familiar potty close at hand. If your child signals the need to use the toilet while you're grocery shopping, it's going to take you about as long to get back to your car as it is to get to the nearest public restroom (if you park strategically, that is). Furthermore, the potty in your car is guaranteed to not be in use. Finally, your child may well balk at sitting on a strange, "big" toilet seat in a strange bathroom (even if you've brought a toilet seat along with you), especially with other people around. Later in this chapter, I'll offer some specific recommendations on how to best accustom your child to the car potty.

SHOW AND TELL: After purchasing your potty or potties, you need to show your child how you (and other family members) use the toilet. For that, you need only leave the bathroom door open and invite him in with you to show him how things are done. Listen up, dads! Until training is over and done with, and your child is no longer showing interest in what you're doing in the bathroom and how you do it, I highly recommend that you sit down to urinate. Have no fear, fellows, this is not going to compromise your masculinity. It's simply good common sense. You're going to want your child—boy or girl—to sit for both "number one" and "number two." If boys (and even some girls) see their dads standing to pee, they're probably going to want to stand to pee, too, and I don't need to describe the likely result.

Parents ask, "Would it be helpful to help prepare my child by reading him a children's potty-training book or having him watch a children's potty-training video?"

It should be obvious by now that I'm a minimalist where toilet training is concerned. Toilet training is no big deal, and anything you do that implies otherwise is going to increase the risk of resistance on the part of your child. So, no, I don't recommend children's potty-training books or videos. To be honest, I think these things are silly at best. Their existence is testimony to pervasive parental anxiety and a corresponding lack of parental confidence where toilet training is concerned. Letting your child watch family members use the toilet and explaining what you're doing in simple terms is sufficient.

DESIGNATE A PRIMARY STAGING AREA: When you begin, the potty or potties should be in plain view. The axiom "out of sight, out of mind" was never so apropos. If your child spends approximately equal time in two rooms—her bedroom and the den, for example—then put one potty in her bedroom and one in the den. If you live in a two-story house, and your child spends significant time on the second level during the day, then I would recommend one potty for each level. I recommend *against* putting the potty in the bathroom.

Some people bristle at that. They contend that a child should learn, from day one, that one "goes to the bathroom" in the bathroom, not in the living room or the den. These folks often reason thus: When a child makes the transition from a crib to a "big bed," the bed stays in the bedroom, where the child sleeps; likewise, when making the transition from diapers to a potty, the potty should be in the bathroom. That's a clever argument, but the two situations are not parallel. You don't have to *teach* a child how to go to sleep. You have to *teach* a child to use a potty. To help your child learn this new skill, it is best to have the potty where it will serve as a near-constant reminder of your new expectations. Having the potty within your usual daytime field of vision also means you're going to know when your child is using it, when she needs help, and when she needs additional guidance. (But if I haven't convinced you, go ahead and put the potty in the bathroom. As you'll soon see, there's more than one way to skin the toilet-training cat.)

A mother recently told me she didn't want the potty in the livingroom because she didn't want her toddler using it in front of houseguests. Okay. That's fine. But I can tell you from personal experience that it's the rare adult who is grossed out by seeing a toddler use a potty. When my now thirty-something daughter Amy was learning to use the potty, we put it in the living room, because that was her preferred play area. She was exactly twenty-four months old when we began training (one of her birthday gifts was a potty) and twenty-four months, one week, when fully trained. During that time, and for several weeks thereafter, whenever one of our friends came over Amy would proudly show them what she was learning. To a person, they thought her explicit demonstrations were nothing but cute. But, as I said, if this seems too strange to you, put the potty in the bathroom. Obsessive–compulsive disorder is nothing to be ashamed of.

As accidents decrease and successes increase, move each (or the) potty in the direction of the nearest bathroom. When two potties are in sight of one another, eliminate one of them. The primary potty might begin its life in the den, then move to the hallway that connects the den to the bathroom, then move down the hallway so it sits right outside the bathroom door, and then move into the bathroom itself.

If you are going to use only one potty, and you are going to put this one potty in the bathroom, so be it. Under the circumstances, it will be out of sight, meaning that your child is going to need periodic reminders about the new expectation. Instead of delivering these reminders yourself, which can quickly devolve into micromanagement and the almost inevitable power struggle that ensues, I strongly recommend that you incorporate the potty bell described in the next chapter, and you may even find that a gate will come in handy, and may even be necessary (again, described in the next chapter).

YOUR SUPPORT SQUAD: Make sure you get your spouse, older siblings who are capable of lending helping hands, relatives who spend time with your child, regular babysitters, and preschool or day care staff on board. Tell each person what you're doing and how they can help. Also, be sensitive to people who don't respond positively to your plan, who try to persuade you to put off training. These are the very people who, if the responsibilities of toilet training suddenly become inconvenient, might put a diaper on your child. If you think one of your child's regular caretakers is likely to do this, try your best to avoid leaving your child with this person until the training is pretty much over.

If your child spends lots of time with a nanny, an in-home sitter, or a family day care provider, it would be advantageous for you to provide that person with a copy of this book and ask them to read it. If they don't have time to read the entire book, then ask them to read this chapter and the next one.

If your child attends a day care program, the staff will probably be very cooperative with you. After all, having a toilet trained child means one less child's diapers to change. Furthermore, toilet training tends to be contagious in toddler groups. One child using the potty elicits the interest of the other children, many of whom begin asking to use the potty, which is a day care center or preschool teacher's dream come true! Although I generally recommend keeping your child at home as much as possible during the first week of training, a fully cooperative, enthusiastic day care or preschool teacher can be your best ally. Let this person know what you intend to do and ask her opinion as to whether your child ought to be home week one or not. If she wants to help, and you trust her, then by all means keep your child in the program. Receiving the same messages about the same expectation from other people with whom your child spends significant time is definitely going to speed the process along.

SIBLING TOILETRY: Back in 1995, my children were five, three, and twenty-one months. One day, my two older girls found a little potty in the basement and proceeded to teach their younger sister how to use it. I was hardly involved at all. The pediatrician was amazed to see her in underwear at her two-year visit. My recommendation for anyone potty training is to involve older siblings. It will free up a lot of your time!

And now, I'll take a couple of questions. Yes, you there, in the back, wearing the lovely banana hat.

Q *I've been trying to toilet train my twenty-six-month-old son for several months. He has a good day, then a few bad days, then a good day, and so on. I'm getting tired of washing training pants! Also, when we leave the house, he wants to wear his Barney pajamas. I have to wrestle "outside" clothes on him. Could it be that he's simply not ready for toilet training?*

A Nah. This is not a problem of readiness. The fact that your son has occasional good days tells me he knows what to do.

Burn the training pants and let him wear his Barney pajamas and his Barney pajamas only, with nothing on underneath. Everywhere: inside, outside, to the shopping center, the opera. Everywhere he goes, Barney goes. Believe me, no one is going to be scandalized by the sight of a toddler in public wearing Barney pajamas, and you aren't going to be reported to the fashion police.

Put the potty out in the open, where he spends most of his time during the day. If that's the living room, so be it. If the potty is out of sight, it's also out of mind. Tell him he can wear his Barney pajamas as long as he doesn't wet them or poop in them. If he wets or poops on Barney, he has to take Barney off so Barney can take a bath, and he can't wear Barney again until Barney is dry. Meanwhile, he has to wear thin cotton underpants. If you want to turn this up a notch, tell him that he can't put Barney back on, even when Barney is dry, until he uses the potty successfully.

This is nothing more than a variation on "Grandma's Rule": When you do what I, the parent, want you to do, you can do what you want to do. You want him to use the potty. He wants a close personal relationship with Barney. Ta-da! Now, next question?

Q *My sixteen-month-old is standing up to pee in his tub every single night, just like clockwork. Also, his bowel movements occur at the same time every day. Thinking we should capitalize on this, we went out and bought a potty. We're not going to push it, but we think it's clear that our little guy is aware of when he's about to relieve himself. We've decided there will be no "Pampers every step of the way" for us, but are we going at this too early?*

A My answer is an unequivocal "No," but before I go on, I need to explain that in 2002, Pampers put out a television ad that featured the slogan "Pampers: Every Step of the Way." Said ad showed a child who looked to be about five or six opening a drawer full of—you got it!—large-size Pampers that were arranged in the drawer like underwear, presumably for the bliss of pulling one out and putting it on by himself. I lampooned the ad in my newspaper column, saying that the way things were going, toilet training would soon become a thing of the past and everyone, regardless of age, would wear disposable diapers and stink equally. I was joking, but I have learned that what is absurd to one person is a marketing opportunity to another.

Now, to your question: No, you would not be going about this too early, not if you're willing to be patient and hang in there. When you start at sixteen months, it may take one to three months for complete success. Generally, boys take longer than girls, so expect three months. That's ninety days. Can you be patient that long? On the other hand, if you wait until your son is, say, twenty months old, he may achieve complete success in one month. In the first case, he'll be trained no later than nineteen months. In the second, he'll be trained at twenty-one months. Obviously, there's a tradeoff involved here that only you can resolve.

PREPARING YOU WITH FIVE C-WORDS

Every good teacher prepares for class in advance. Toilet training requires that you teach, and the effectiveness of your teaching will depend in large part on how effectively you plan ahead. Arrange things so that you are able to remain at home as much as possible during the first week of training. Do that week's grocery shopping, and other errands you can anticipate having to do, beforehand. If you work outside the home, take vacation or personal time. This all but ensures that you will be able to stay focused on the task at hand and provide a consistent learning environment for your child. Do not go into this with the intent of being finished within a week, because you probably won't be. However, a week of focused but relaxed training should get the project off the ground and to a point where your child is cruising fairly smoothly toward the finish line. Most important, you absolutely must approach toilet training with the understanding that once you get started you are going to see it through until completion. An attitude of "we'll try this for a while and see if it works out" is almost surely going to doom the project to failure.

In fact, your attitude is the most important variable of all. A proper attitude consists of five Cs: cool, calm, collected, confident, and committed.

COOL means that you approach this as if it's the most natural thing in the world to be doing at this point in time—no big deal. Keep in mind that toilet training is no bigger a deal than teaching your child to feed himself with a spoon: You demonstrate, give whatever assistance is needed, and clean up the messes the child will make during the learning process. Let's consider a comparison: You don't agonize over whether your child is ready to begin learning to use a spoon; you can see with your own eyes that he is capable of holding a spoon and guiding it, however clumsily, to his mouth. You accept that a certain amount of trial and error is going to be involved, and you resolve to be patient. You don't peruse the library for books on spoon training. At most, you might call your mother and ask her for some practical advice. You don't buy him a spoon that plays Tchaikovsky's "1812 Overture" when he manages to get it into his mouth without spilling its contents. You don't read your child picture books or show him videos of children using spoons. You don't jump up and down and clap and squeal the first time your child gets the spoon to his mouth successfully. You just say, "Good for you!" and let that be it. You don't reward him with stars or new toys for feeding himself. You let the mastery of the skill be its own reward. And so it should be with toilet training. Now, say this out loud: "And so it *will* be!"

CALM means that you communicate your expectations without fanfare or anxiety, and respond to accidents without drama—and remember, you most surely are going to deal with accidents, because every learning process is a matter of trial and *error*.

COLLECTED means your approach to the toilet-training project is organized, not haphazard. If necessary, reread the previous section of this chapter ("The Preliminaries").

CONFIDENT means you are absolutely certain of success and that you communicate that certainty to your child in a cool, calm, and collected manner.

Finally, **COMMITTED** means you are going to see this through to completion. You are not going to do what so many parents do: After starting toilet training, they experience more failure (accidents) than success, and so they stop and put their child back in diapers; they wait awhile, then they start again, but again, they experience more failure than success, so they stop; they wait awhile, and so on. This on again, off again approach often results in a child of three or older who is still in diapers and who, furthermore, has now become wary of and therefore resistant to the idea of sitting on the toilet, because toilet training has been, to this point, as much of a hassle for him as it has been for his mother.

It is going to make things much easier if you find a primary support person who will stand by your side (figuratively, of course) for the duration of training. This person can be your mother, your best friend (or a group of friends), your spouse (I surely hope that your spouse is as committed to this as you are and willing to pitch in and help), or your child's day care teacher—someone you can ask for advice, someone who will be encouraging, someone you can turn to if the going gets rough. Without such support, you are more likely to cave in at the first sign that things are not going exactly as planned. If you don't have someone who fits the bill within your network of family and friends, use this book or the members' side of my Web site (www.rosemond.com) as your support system. There, you'll find close to one thousand questions Diane and I have answered about toilet training. In addition, members can access every newspaper column I've ever written on the subject.

AN UNSOLICITED TESTIMONIAL: I began potty training my twenty-four-month-old twin boys last week, even though both grandmothers told me that because they were premature and walked late, twenty-four months was too early. The first two days were totally unsuccessful. They sat on the potty every thirty minutes but without success. I remained calm and explained each time they wet the floor that their pee and poop belong in the potty. The third day I was ready to give up, thinking maybe the grandmothers had been right. Then I logged onto www.rosemond.com and read about one hundred potty-training questions/answers and testimonials, all of which inspired me to persevere. Here we are a week later, and they are nearly accident free! They are still naked, and we need to add pants, etc., but we are well on our way. Thanks for the encouragement and information!

Please don't set a specific time frame as a goal, as in "my child will be toilet trained within two weeks." A goal of that sort is going to cause you to feel pressured and anxious, and you are not going to be able to help communicating that pressure and anxiety to your child. The inevitable result: a child who balks at using the potty. Once you incorporate the Five Cs into your attitude, you have to go with the flow. (Am I clever with the puns or what?) If you set a specific date as a goal, you will most surely become a control freak where toilet training is concerned, unable to relax because you will be thinking constantly of a date that is looming ever closer.

ANOTHER TANTRUM-FREE MOM: My twins—a boy and a girl—both learned to use the potty at the same time, with no older siblings, no day care peers, and by a developmental age of twenty months (they were eight weeks premature). They are now twenty-two months old, and I consider them 90 percent trained. Neither is very verbal, but they have ways of telling me they have to go. If we can do it, just about anyone can!

THE WHOLE POOP ON "NAKED AND $75"

Okay, enough talk. Let's get down to business. (The pun possibilities are endless, aren't they?) The first question you should be asking is, "What does 'Naked and $75' mean, anyway?"

"Naked" means that during the actual training phase your child is going to be naked or, if a boy, wearing thin cotton underpants only. "$75" means that after your child has mastered using the toilet, you are going to call a carpet cleaner and pay approximately $75 to have him remove the stains and smell from your carpets. Although human urine doesn't smell or stain nearly as badly as animal urine, you should do your best to remove accidents as they happen. I recommend a cleaner made for dog and cat stains. Better safe than sorry. No matter how fastidious you are, however, I'd still recommend a professional steam cleaning and deodorizing after you cross the finish line. (Remember that the smells in your house are more evident to someone who doesn't live with them every day.)

"Naked and $75" consists of seven components or considerations:

FIRST, SET THE STAGE PROPERLY. Put your child's potty out in the open, in the area of the house where she spends most of her time during the day. Yes, even if that means the living room.

"Mommy and Daddy have a potty of their very own, and Big Sister has a potty of her very own, and now you have a potty of your very own! Isn't that exciting!?"

Believe me, and I speak from experience, a potty in the middle of the living room is a great conversation piece. And should your child come into the living room and want to sit on her potty while you have someone over, so be it. Make a potty party of the occasion!

"Hey! Look here! Alberta is going to show us how she uses the potty! She started using it three days ago and is doing great!"

If the person has any sense of humor at all, he or she will pick up on the cue and chime in with something like "Yes! That is great, isn't it? Alberta! You're such a big girl! You'll be driving and dating in no time!"

I'm kidding about the driving and dating comment, but you get the idea. I can't stress enough that I do not recommend keeping the potty hidden in the bathroom, which is where most people are inclined to keep it. The fact that the potty is out in the open, where the child spends the majority of her time, means that it will serve as a constant visual reminder of what's now being expected of her. If you insist, for whatever reason, that the potty be kept in the bathroom, read on.

Setting the stage properly also means getting rid of diapers, pull-ups, the changing table, and anything else that is associated with wearing diapers. All this stuff should disappear from view. Get it out of the house! Give it away to a pregnant friend. Keeping the accoutrements of a prior era around will only tempt you to turn back to them if the going gets the least bit rough. If you give up smoking but you keep a pack of cigarettes in the top drawer of your bedside table "just in case," you will surely be back to smoking within a month. The same is true of keeping diapers "on reserve" when you are toilet training.

SECOND, COMMUNICATE YOUR EXPECTATIONS CLEARLY. In my seminars, I always place great stress on the fact that a parent's effectiveness as a disciplinarian depends more on how well the parent communicates expectations than on how well the parent manipulates reward and punishment (consequences). For most parents, toilet training is the first big disciplinary step they will take with their children. Therefore, it is very important that good disciplinary precedents be established during the toilet-training process, and the most important of these precedents involves the proper use of what I call Leadership Speech, or speech that is consistent with three more "C" words:

- CONCISE: Leadership speech is brief and straightforward. It is fairly devoid of explanations, because when parents explain themselves to their children, they are likely to sound as if they are trying to persuade their children to cooperate rather than expecting them to obey. It is "I need you to pick up these toys and move them to another room," as opposed to "I have some friends coming over, and we need to use this room, so let's try and get these toys picked up, okay?"

- CLEAR: The more concise a parent's instructions, the more clear they will be, but clarity is also greatly enhanced when you give instructions and convey expectations to your child using concrete rather than abstract terms. This is clear: "I want you to hold my hand while we're in the store." This is not: "I want you to stay close to me while we're in the store." How close is close, especially when the person who is supposed to stay "close" is a young child?

- COMMANDING: When parents use leadership speech, it is clear that they are giving instructions and not asking questions. By the way, I find that when parents use leadership speech effectively, they rarely find themselves having to resort to demands. Put another way, parents who frequently *demand* things of their children are parents who have not learned how to *command*.

The opposite of Leadership Speech is Milquetoast Speech, named after the main character in a popular comic strip that ran from 1924 to 1953. Caspar Milquetoast was the archetypal wimp. He acquiesced to just about anything and never spoke with any confidence. Unfortunately, all too many of today's parents, when they talk to their children, have a habit of using Milquetoast Speech:

> *Parent bends over in an attempt to put her face at the same level as the child's, puts her hands on her knees, conjures up a "gee whiz!" facial expression, and says, with great enthusiasm, "Would you like to try something new today? I bought you this potty so you could learn to use it just like Mommy and Daddy! When you sit on it, it plays your favorite song! Would you like to sit on it and try to poop or pee right now? I'll bring some cookies over, and we can have a potty party! What do you say?"*

The child in question has every reason to think something is up, and for that reason this is exactly the sort of overly enthusiastic approach that is almost sure to provoke a worried look and a lack of cooperation, if not downright defiance. Here's the same parent, using Leadership Speech:

> *Parent, from a fully upright, and therefore authoritative, position, says (with matter-of-fact tone), "Today, you're going to learn to sit on this potty to poop and pee, just like Mommy and Daddy sit on the big potty in the bathroom when we poop and pee. Come over here, and I'll show you how to sit on it."*

My parents described speech of this sort as "short and sweet." I think "sweet" referred to the fact that it is almost certain to produce results.

THIRD, MAKE IT AS SIMPLE AS POSSIBLE FOR YOUR CHILD. This is where "naked" comes in. Let your child walk around the house naked or, in the case of a boy, wearing only the thinnest cotton underwear you can find. The idea—are you ready for this?—is to have the "stuff" run down the child's legs. That's right! In order to replace the old habit—eliminating whenever and wherever she feels the urge—with a new habit—using the potty—the cues associated with the old habit must be eliminated as much as possible. One of those cues is bulky, absorbent material around the child's pelvic area, material that is associated with letting go without concern for place or time. Another way of saying this: *To help your child learn something new, you need to get rid of the old.* Also, by letting your child walk around naked from the waist down (or wearing thin underpants), she will immediately know when she has an accident, and so will you. When she feels the discomfort of "stuff" running or oozing (I hope that's not too rudely graphic) down her legs, she will stand stock still, spread her legs, look down, get a horrified look on her face, and begin to yell. Hearing her, you will arrive on the scene as soon as possible, probably while she's still in the act.

If so, you should say, with cool, calm, confidence, "Let's get you cleaned up, and let's get the floor cleaned up. But first, listen to me. When you feel poo-poo or pee-pee about to happen, you need to go sit down on the potty, which is right over there," or something along those lines, something that is not scolding or critical but coolly and calmly directive.

FOURTH, RESPOND PROPERLY TO MISTAKES. Obviously, I ran a bit ahead of myself in the last paragraph, but it seemed awkward to break that description into two parts. The first thing to keep in mind about mistakes, accidents, whatever you call them, is—and I cannot emphasize this enough—*they are inevitable!* When they happen, respond matter-of-factly (e.g., "You had an accident, so let's get you cleaned up"), encouragingly ("I know you'll do better next time"), and instructively ("The next time you feel a poo-poo, go sit on your potty like Mommy showed you" or "Remember that pee and poop go in the potty"). Needless to say, yelling and other outbursts of frustration on your part are going to be counterproductive.

After an accident, the first thing to do is not what you are probably inclined to do, which is to clean up the mess. Instead, take advantage of the teaching opportunity the accident has presented. Remember that a toddler's attention span is very short, just slightly longer than a puppy's, in fact. If you deal with the mess first, you lose the teaching opportunity, and your child learns, "When I pee on the floor, mommy cleans it up."

If you discover an accident and don't know when it occurred, lead your child over to it and be very clear about your expectations, as in, "Your pee/poop does not belong on the floor. It belongs in the potty. Go sit on the potty right now and see if you can poop or pee some more for Mommy."

Yes, you can actually talk in this straightforward fashion to a toddler and not destroy his little psyche. Again, you're not angry, but you need to be somewhat stern. You definitely want to convey disapproval, and you definitely want to be clear about your expectations. Talk of the following sort just doesn't get it: "Well, we had an accident, didn't we? That's all right. Mommy will clean it up. Try and do better next time, okay?"

You can also deal with accidents by using what is known as the Socratic method—in other words, by asking questions:

- "Where is your pee/poop supposed to go?"

- "Where is your potty? Show me."

- "What do you do if you need help?"

If your child doesn't immediately answer, then answer for him:

- "In the potty."

- "In your playroom. That's right, right over there."

- "Call Mommy or Daddy."

And then ask him the question again and praise him when he is able to answer correctly: "That's right! You know what to do!" Getting your child to state the answers to these essential questions will strengthen his awareness of your expectations and bring about quicker success.

The occasional child asks for help every time he needs to sit, even though the help is really not needed. This is probably a personality thing. Some children take boldly to new situations and challenges, and some, by nature, are more reticent and need more time to scope them out before tackling them on their own. If your child asks for help, give it, at least at first. Keep in mind that if he's asking for your help, he *wants* to use the potty. Not a problem! You certainly don't want to frustrate him at this critical point. But whereas you initially give the help he asks for (even if you don't think he really needs it), you will want to slowly wean him. You can do this by simply giving less and less help over a two-week period. At first, you help him out of his underpants and hold him steady while he backs up to and sits on the potty. Then you pull his underwear halfway down and have him pull them off the rest of the way, but you still hold him steady. The next step involves walking him to his potty and having him take his underpants off, but you still hold him steady, and so on. In two weeks, maybe even less, he'll be feeling confident enough to do everything on his own. By the way, it's a good idea to put the potty next to a piece of sturdy furniture that he can hold onto when he goes to sit. The less you have to do for him, the better.

If your child starts grunting and gets that scrunched facial expression that signals an impending bowel movement, don't hesitate to direct him to the potty. If he doesn't move, then by all means pick him up and take him there as quickly as you can. Get him seated and walk away, saying, "Call me when you're done, and I'll help you dump it in the big potty." If you see telltale signs of elimination (the scrunched look, squeezing the legs together, pulling at or holding the genitals) don't ask, "Do you have to use the potty?" Remember the need for authoritative speech and say, "You need to use the potty. Go sit." (As opposed to something along the irresolute lines of, "Do you need to use the potty? Let's go sit on it and try to do something, okay?")

What if you see your child blatantly emptying his bladder or bowels on the floor? First, try your best to refrain from shrieking or rushing toward him with arms outstretched. A sharp "Hey!" may be enough to cause him to clamp it off, at least momentarily. Then, even if he's finished, direct him to sit on the potty: "I told you, your poop/pee does not go on the floor. Go sit on the potty and see if you can make more." Again, you need to be stern, but not angry.

FIFTH, RESPOND PROPERLY TO SUCCESSES. You wouldn't think people need to be told how to respond to a child who successfully uses the potty on her own or pretty much on her own, but they do. The most common mistake parents—especially those who read parenting books—make in this situation is to praise too much. I'm talking about the parent who, when her child uses the potty successfully, acts like she just won the jackpot on *Jeopardy*. She jumps up and down, clapping her hands, squealing with delight. To top it off, she runs into the kitchen and comes back with a plate of cookies or some other reward for her child. To be sure, this is all very well intentioned; nonetheless, it is as counterproductive as losing one's temper when one's child has an accident.

Keeping your cool and remaining calm applies to toilet-training successes as much as it does failures. Making a big deal of your child's successes is going to be as detrimental as making a big deal of his failures.

In both cases, the problem is making a big deal of something that isn't a big deal. Making a big deal of success puts a child in the spotlight, and the minute a child is in the spotlight, resistance becomes more likely, no matter the issue. So when your child has success, praise him, but make it *cool* praise, as in, "Hey! Good job! Isn't that fun? And isn't it nice that you don't have to wear diapers anymore? Yep, it sure is!"

For most kids, the simple act of carrying the potty to the bathroom, emptying it in the "big potty," and flushing it down is going to be reinforcement enough. Don't do what one author of child care books advises: Reward your child's success with candy, gum, and shopping trips.

Someone, somewhere, is asking, "But what's wrong with rewarding successes with small pieces of candy or cookies?"

Two things: First, researchers have found that rewarding children for proper behavior often backfires. I suspect that rewards and "hot" praise both tip a child off to the fact that the issue—in this case, toilet training—is something very important to the parent. Many a toddler, having come to this intuitive realization, will become oppositional. Why? Because—and if you've lived with a toddler, this will come as nothing new—toddlers have a strange and vexing way of resisting anything and everything that they sense is important to their parents, and the more important something is to a parent, the more a toddler is likely to resist.

The other thing about using rewards is that a child will "saturate" on any given reward very quickly. At the point of having had his fill of the reward, he just might stop producing the desired behavior. It's almost as if the child says to herself, "I don't want a cookie right now, so I'll just poop right here, on the floor." You want your child to figure out for herself that using the toilet successfully—thus, being dry and clean—is its own best reward. Don't distract her from this realization with candy or toys.

SIXTH, DON'T PROVIDE ENTERTAINMENT. I am *not* in favor of parents entertaining (reading, singing, playing games) or giving junk food to children while they are on the potty. Approaches of that sort just aren't natural; rather, they reflect parental anxiety and insecurity. For one thing, both entertainment and the "potty party" require that the parent be present while the child is sitting. That's a recipe for increasing micromanagement. Furthermore, entertainment is likely to distract your child from the task at hand and result in a potty-sitting marathon that lasts fifteen to sixty minutes and ends without success.

If when your child sits on the potty she takes the toy she was playing with, fine. But don't turn potty-sitting into something it isn't and was never intended to be.

"But, John," a parent once argued, "when I sit on the toilet, I often read something. What's the difference if I read something to my child when *she* sits on the potty?"

The difference is that you read to yourself, someone does not sit in the bathroom with you, reading to you. Furthermore, you know what your primary purpose is; reading to yourself is simply a means of passing the time. Reading to a child while she's sitting on the potty is likely to be a distraction. Likewise, you can suggest to your child that she put a few of her favorite books next to the potty and "read" them while she sits, but don't do her entertaining for her.

Example: "Sometimes, when I sit on the potty, I read a book or a magazine until I'm done. If you want to read while you sit, just like Mommy, we can put some of your favorite books over there next to your potty."

See how natural, relaxed, and casual that is? I'll say it again, because I probably can't say it enough: Keeping the business of toilet training as natural, relaxed, and casual as possible is going to make for quicker success. Think of this as "green" or "organic" toilet training. No unnecessary or artificial ingredients. (Note: Because of the previous two sentences, this book is now in compliance with

Federal Statute 15.359 of the Completely Counterproductive Code, and anyone reading it can apply for tax credits through the Bureau of Redundancy.)

SHE TOLD HIM, AND THAT WAS THAT: When my son was almost twenty-two months old, I got up one morning and simply told him that we were through with diapers during the daytime. I was ready for him to learn to use the potty, and I explained this in very clear terms. He mastered it fairly quickly, which I don't find to be such a remarkable thing, but I am astonished at the number of people who have expressed surprise that a boy got the hang of it at such an "early" age.

SEVENTH, KEEP YOUR DISTANCE. There is nothing that will more surely doom toilet training to frustration and failure for both parent and child than parental micromanagement, as in well-intentioned attempts to prevent the child from making mistakes. One of the reasons you are going to let your child walk around naked or almost naked is so you (hopefully) don't have to assist her in sitting on the potty, so that any involvement on your part can be minimal. The less involved you are, the more effectively you let your child own the process. Consequently, the more pride she is going to take in her successes. Micromanaging your child during toilet training—trying to prevent accidents—will frustrate your child's attempts to master the process. After all, how can you master a new task when someone else is constantly interrupting the normal, natural trial-and-*error* of your learning?

Ironically, the parent who hovers anxiously over the child, constantly reminding the child to remember to sit on the potty, obsessively trying to get the child to sit "for just a little while to see if anything happens," and so on, is going to provoke resistance (toddlers want to do *everything* themselves, so the trick here is to give them enough space, along with enough guidance, to make them think they're doing this completely on their own). The child's resistance is going to provoke frustration on the part of the parent, maybe even outbursts of anger, and the child is going to respond by becoming even more resistant, whether passively or actively.

Testimony from a mom who realized that she was micromanaging: "When my first son was twenty-seven months I began potty training with the 'Naked and $75' method. However, I couldn't relax about it. I was always hanging around him, trying to prevent accidents. For about six weeks he was successful some of the time but still had periodic accidents. Then I read one of your articles on the need to avoid micromanagement during training, and I was shocked. You were writing about me! I heeded your advice, and my son had very few accidents after that."

Okay, that's it. You now have your attitude straight and all the set pieces in place.

LET'S GET STARTED!

THE FIRST MINUTE OF THE FIRST HOUR OF THE FIRST DAY: You've made up your mind. You've decided whether to go with potty seats or potty chairs (or a combination thereof), and you've decided where you're going to place them. For the last few weeks, you and your husband, and perhaps even older siblings, have let your child watch you go to the bathroom. The night before the not-so-big day, after your child went to sleep, you made everything associated with diapers disappear. You've tossed and turned all night long, bathed in sweat, worrying that something is going to go wrong, that this is going to blow up in your face. No, not really. You've read this book and you've wrapped yourself in the Five Cs: cool, calm, collected, confident, and committed. Nothing can stop you now!

Your child wakes up in the morning. You greet him, lift him out of his crib, lay him down, and remove his diaper. When you're done, you put only the thinnest (make sure they're really flimsy) cotton underwear on him. If your child is a girl, you leave her naked from the waist down. You take a deep breath, and you say, "You're not wearing diapers anymore, Reginald (or Regina). Today, Mommy and Daddy are going to teach you how to use the potty. Come with me and I'll show you."

You put him down, take his hand, and take him to the nearest potty. You say, "This is your potty. It's just like Mommy and Daddy's, only smaller. You've seen Mommy and Daddy poop and pee on the potty, and now it's time for you to start pooping and peeing on your very own potty. I want you to sit on it and see how it feels. That's great! Most excellent! From now on, when you feel like you have to poop or pee, you just sit on this potty. If you need help, call Mommy or Daddy and we'll help you. Okay, I'm going to go fix your breakfast now. While I'm fixing breakfast, see if you can poop or pee in your new potty."

And you're off and running!

A WORD TO THE WISE ABOUT THE "BOY" PROBLEM: It goes without saying that the parents of a boy will need to teach him to push his penis down while on the potty, so that his urine goes into the potty and not straight out over the top (splash guards are meant to prevent this, but they are not always effective and sometimes a sitting hazard). If your son insists on standing like he's seen Daddy do, don't stand in his way! If that's the case, you may want to locate the potty in the bathroom or a room that's not carpeted. Even so, put towels on the floor around the potty chair. This is obviously a messier way to go, but if your little fellow wants to do it this way, it's worth letting him have his way as opposed to getting into a power struggle over sitting.

NO "BOY PROBLEM" HERE: When my son was twenty-two months old we put him in "big boy" underwear and didn't look back. Everyone told me it couldn't be done because boys younger than two-and-one-half or three don't have the necessary self-control or emotional maturity (talk about the "dumbing down" of the American male!). The first four days were very difficult, but he caught on very quickly. I'm proud to say that not only was my son trained before his second birthday but he was also an inspiration to other moms.

STAY THE COURSE! At this point, and even periodically until you're out of the proverbial woods, I recommend that you reread this chapter. The occasional refresher course will help you maintain adherence to the program. If you begin to experience problems that haven't been discussed, don't fret. I know what the potential problems are, and I'll tell you how to solve them in the next chapter.

If you initiate, and your child resists, ask yourself whether you're anxious. Again, parental anxiety results in micromanagement (e.g., nervous questions like, "Do you need to use the potty?" and "Let's go try to use the potty again, okay?"), and that is the number-one cause of child resistance. If you're on pins and needles, it's time to remind yourself that teaching a child to use the toilet is no more worthy of anxiety than teaching a child to feed himself with a spoon. Take a deep breath, calm down, and reread this chapter.

Also, give it time. Rome wasn't built in a day, and Reginald or Regina is rarely trained in a week. If after a few days, your naked or barely covered child is still having more accidents than successes, or just doesn't seem to be getting it, don't jump to the conclusion that he's not ready or some such foolishness. Stay the course. Some kids get it right away and some don't. Some take three days to train, and some are still pooping and peeing all over the place after three days. Stay the course. Have I said that enough?

However, if you stay the course for a week and are not seeing any progress, or your child takes one step forward and then one step back and then one step forward and so on, it's definitely time to up the ante, to apply some benign pressure to the process. The whens and hows of that are described in the next chapter, but don't take things out of order. No matter what, read the rest of this chapter first.

THE TRANSITION TO A POTTY SEAT: When training is pretty much over and done with, you can transition to a padded toilet seat, but again, set things up so that your child needs as little help from you as possible. Where there is a toilet seat, there should be a stool so he can get up on the toilet himself. And when you get to that stage, he'll no longer be naked; he'll be wearing clothing. Make sure it's loose fitting and elastic waisted so he can pull down his own pants with ease. I recommend that the child go from naked below the waist or, for boys, thin cotton underpants only, to loose-fitting shorts without underpants, to elastic-waisted long pants without underpants, to long pants with underpants, after which you should be shouting for joy. Transitioning to a toilet seat at home will also help your child feel more comfortable sitting on a "big potty" in public restrooms and other people's houses.

This from a mom who has done it both ways: "I trained my older daughter on the big toilet. The plus side was that she would go wherever we were without being intimidated by any kind of toilet. The down side was that someone had to take her when she had to go until she was nearly four years old because she was short, and it was difficult for her to get on and off by herself. My second daughter was trained on a toddler-size potty. She really prefers not to use the big one, and when we are out she prefers to wait and hold it until we get home, where she goes in her own little potty. I hardly ever have to prompt her or help her. The little potty is very portable, and we take it with us to Grandma's when we visit. After doing it both ways, I can say there are pluses and minuses to both, but I prefer the little potty. Soon enough my second daughter will be big enough to switch to the big toilet, and she will already have the independence gained from using the little one on her own."

WHEN YOU LEAVE THE HOUSE: Until your child has transitioned to a potty seat at home, you really cannot expect him to use a public toilet, and *you most definitely do not want to put him back in diapers or pull-ups when you leave your house.* So, until that transition has been made, I recommend you take his potty with you and be proactive about its use. Don't wait until your child signals the need to go and then dash madly to your car. Instead, when you arrive at your destination, say, "Before we go into the store, you need to sit on the potty." Don't ask, "Do you need to use the potty before we go into the store?" The latter, being a question, is not authoritative. It is equivocal, and is likely to evoke, "No!" Remember that you're going to be dealing with a toddler, and toddlers, even some who are younger than two, take every opportunity possible to use their favorite word.

If your toddler sits on the "car potty" for a few minutes and nothing happens, then go into the store, first reminding him, "Tell me if you feel a (whatever you call it)." Fifteen to thirty minutes into the shopping trip, say, "It's time to try and use the potty again," and head for the car. Again, don't say, "Do you feel anything?" or "Are you ready to try using the potty again?" or "It's time to use the potty again, okay?" Declare the intent, proceed to your car, put your child on the potty, and stand aside. Read something. Sing a song to yourself while contemplating the clouds (I recommend songs with images of water, like "Raindrops Keep Fallin' on My Head" or "Up a Lazy River"). In any case, don't stand there anxiously like you're waiting to find out whether you won the lottery. You may have to take your child to the car several times before something happens. A tip: During times like this, it helps to have your child drink lots of water. Water, mind you, not soda or anything sugar sweetened. Drinks of that sort don't "run through" one as quickly. They're bad for your child, anyway.

Okay, folks, that's the full story on N75. My finding has been that when parents properly initiate and manage the program, most children will be successfully trained in three to six weeks. But *most* is not all. Two or three out of ten will be having problems of one sort or another, including acting like they don't understand and even actively rebelling. That's when the potty bell, "the Doctor," and the gate come into play.

4

BELL, DOC, AND BARRIER

Over the course of raising two children and counseling thousands of parents, both face-to-face and through my Web site at www. rosemond.com, I've discovered three aids to toilet training that have helped ease and expedite the process for many a parent and child. These are the potty bell, "the Doctor," and the gate. I offer them here for your consideration. If I were doing this all over again with my children, and especially my son, I'd definitely go with the potty bell and "the Doctor" right off the bat, and take a wait-and-see with regard to the gate. Where your child is concerned, trust your intuition.

THE POTTY BELL

A potty bell, which is nothing more than a small kitchen timer that emits an audible sound of one sort or another (preferably a buzzer or sustained tone) when a set time has expired, can help you organize your approach to toilet training, focus your child on the task at hand, reduce the likelihood of resistance, and help you avoid the inclination to micromanage. The concept is quite simple and practical: The timer signals to the child that it's time to sit on the potty. By using an impersonal signal, it defuses any tendency on your child's part to resist. *You* aren't telling your child to sit; the timer is.

Put the timer in the designated toilet-training area, where your child can hear it when it rings or buzzes. Set it to go off after a certain amount of time has elapsed. I generally recommend an interval of sixty to ninety minutes, but as training unfolds, you can adjust the interval to more closely match your child's rhythms. You can also alter the interval to take special circumstances into consideration. For example, if your child usually has a bowel movement twenty to thirty minutes after he eats lunch, then set the first after-lunch interval at twenty minutes. To increase the likelihood that your child will experience success when he sits on the potty, I recommend that you have him drink more water than usual. (If your child doesn't like water, you are probably allowing him to drink sugary drinks such as fruit juices and fruit-flavored punches. If that's the case, then before you begin toilet training, begin diluting his usual liquids with water and increasing the proportion over a two-week period until he is drinking pure water or water that is only slightly flavored.) Be careful! A parent who is anxious about messes on the floor may be inclined to set an interval that is too brief, reducing the child's chance of success. If the potty bell rings and your child sits and produces nothing after five minutes or so, then tell him to get up. Give him some water and reset the timer for thirty minutes, maybe less. Trust your intuition about this. The important thing is that your child experience success fairly early in the game. Finding a suitable interval for your child will involve some initial trial and error.

Introduce your child to the potty bell by telling him something along these lines: "This is a potty bell. It tells children when to sit on the potty. When it rings, that means you need to go sit on the potty until you poop or pee. I'm going to put the potty bell right here so that you can hear it."

A simple explanation is best. Set the timer for the interval you've decided on. When it rings, direct your child to sit on the potty in a casual yet commanding fashion: "There's the potty bell! That means you need to go sit on the potty."

Because your child is naked, or almost so, he shouldn't need any help from you. (If he's a boy, have him take his underpants off completely rather than just pull them down, and show him beforehand how to sit with the pee guard removed and then insert the pee guard himself.) When he's seated himself successfully, your job is to go find something, anything, to do so you don't hover anxiously over him, waiting for him to produce something. As you walk away, say something like, "Let me know when you've pooped or peed so that I can help you put it in the big potty." By walking away, by giving your child the space he needs to feel independent, you not only communicate your confidence to him, but you also activate a very important toilet-training axiom: The more successful you are at letting go of the urge to hover, the more successful your child will be at letting go.

When the bell rings, do not say something like, "There's the potty bell! Do you feel like sitting on the potty?" or "How about let's try and sit on the potty now, okay?" Those are examples of Milquetoast (wimp) speech, not leadership speech, and I can't stress strongly enough that the former increases the likelihood of resistance.

Initially, you're going to have to prompt your child to remember what to do when the potty bell rings (and some children may need a more authoritative prompt or more help than others), but if you let your child own the learning that's taking place, it should not take more than a few days before prompts will be completely unnecessary; your child will hear the bell and immediately go sit on the potty.

Here are the two primary advantages to using the potty bell:

- Because the signal to go sit on the potty is coming from an impersonal source as opposed to you, any tendency your child may have to resist is minimized, if not completely neutralized.

- Any tendency on your part to vigilantly hover and anxiously ask, every few minutes, "Do you have to sit on the potty?" is likewise minimized, if not completely eliminated.

Thus, toilet training's two biggest stumbling blocks—resistance from the child and micromanagement on the part of the parent—

are removed, thus clearing the way for your child to feel that he is in control of the process and that his successes are his and his alone. Mastery is made of this. Within a short time that may vary from a few days to a few weeks, your child will figure out that certain internal sensations mean he needs to eliminate, and he will begin sitting on the potty and producing independent of a prompt from the potty bell. At that point, the training is off the ground, and you can put the potty bell away for your next child.

THE POTTY BELL SAVES THE DAY: I decided it was time to potty train my son when he was twenty-one months old. I took Friday and Monday off from work so I could give it my undivided attention for four days. After lots of accidents, and realizing that I was becoming frustrated, I began using the potty bell, setting it to ring every hour, on the hour. The first time it rang, he needed me to tell him what to do, but he had success. A few weeks later, he was completely trained, and he was dry in the morning to boot! The potty bell is a great idea!

THIS DOC MAKES HOUSE CALLS

Children—even infants and young toddlers—are studious observers of human behavior, and especially the behavior of adults. They notice things we don't think they notice, and they understand much more than they can express with language. For example, by the time your child is eighteen months of age, he has figured out that his doctor's authority trumps your own. He has seen that when the doctor comes into the examining room, you defer to him and become compliant. Furthermore, when you and your child are back home and you are carrying out the doctor's instructions, you often remind him that "the doctor said this" and "the doctor said that" to explain what you are doing.

Your child's recognition of his doctor's authority can be used to great advantage during toilet training. By strategically invoking the authority of the doctor, you can further diminish the possibility that your child will become resistant in response to your instructions and expectations. Examples:

- "Your doctor says it's time for you to begin learning how to use the potty."

- "Your doctor says that when the potty bell rings, you have to sit on the potty until you poop or you pee."

- "Your doctor says that until you learn to use the potty, he wants you to be naked (or only wear underpants) while you're at home."

- "Your doctor says you need to drink a lot of water while you're learning to use the potty."

- "I talked to your doctor today, and he says you're doing a great job of using the potty!"

"The Doctor" is a handy person to have around. I routinely recommend that whether the issue is bedtime, meals, clothing, or picking up toys, parents who are dealing with a strong-willed toddler simply state the instruction in terms of "this is what the Doctor wants." Almost without exception, parents report great success with it; they're often amazed at how the mere mention of the Doctor so completely disarms their children's resistance.

- "Your doctor says that this is when you have to go to bed."

- "Your doctor says you can't sleep with us anymore."

- "I talked to your doctor today, and he says you have to wear long pants to school."

- "Your doctor told me that when we eat together as a family, you have to eat the same things Mommy and Daddy eat."

- "When you finish playing with your toys, you have to pick them up. Your doctor says so."

Every so often someone complains to me that this is the same as lying to a child. Invoking the Doctor's authority may not be an absolute truth, but it is definitely is not in the same category as a devious and dastardly lie. In the first place, you are telling the child to do something that is in his best interest. A lie is told for the benefit of the liar. The Doctor is invoked for the benefit of the child. Second, you're not concealing important information from your child. Third, your child's doctor would almost certainly approve of your expectations.

Several parents have asked, "Won't this cause a child to lose trust in you when he discovers that the doctor didn't really say all those things?"

Does finding out that the Tooth Fairy is fantasy cause a child to lose trust in his parents? The same can be asked of Santa Claus, the Easter Bunny, and the Sandman. In every case, the answer is no. If there is an already existing lack of trust on the child's part, the discovery that Santa Claus is not the bringer of Christmas gifts or the Tooth Fairy is not the benefactor who leaves money under the pillow may tip the scale, but in and of themselves these discoveries do not damage the parent–child relationship. As is the case with Santa Claus and the Tooth Fairy, by the time a child discovers that the Doctor is nothing but a playful idea that served a certain purpose, the child will be old enough to appreciate the humor involved.

Some folks worry that invoking the Doctor might cause a child to develop fears about the real thing. The proof is in the pudding: I have never, not once, heard from a parent who invoked the Doctor that her child became afraid of the real, flesh-and-blood doctor. It goes without saying that it's wrongly manipulative and downright mean for a desperate parent to say something along the lines of, "Your doctor says if you don't pick up your toys I have to spank you!" but most people, and this is especially true of people who read books of this sort, have more common sense than to use the Doctor to scare their kids into obedience. Finally, not one of the dozens of pediatricians and family practitioners I've spoken to about this innocent mythmaking has objected, and many of them have thought it was rather funny.

TO THE BARRICADES!

A childproof safety gate is a handy way of partitioning off and thus keeping your child in the designated toilet-training area. Restricting the child's "field of freedom" during training ensures that he doesn't lose sight of the new expectation. It also makes the job of supervision a lot easier for you.

A gate can also come in handy if your child is resistant toward the notion of sitting on the potty or seems completely uninterested. Neither resistance nor lack of interest indicates that your child isn't ready. Some children may balk at the notion of sitting on the potty simply because it's something new. Some children may balk simply because on the day their parents begin their training, they woke up on the wrong side of the bed, disinclined to cooperate with anything their parents asked of them. At the other end of the reaction spectrum are the occasional kids who, when introduced to the potty, act like it's not there. It's the rare child who doesn't seem to mind stuff running down his or her legs, but it happens. Whether random resistance or disinterest, we're not talking about a problem having to do with the training itself or lack of readiness but rather the nature of the toddler. In either case, a gate is the solution.

A gate can be used in one of two ways:

- To cordon off a certain area. For example, if you've decided to put the potty in the doorway between the play room and the family room because that's where your toddler spends most of his or her time during the day, then use a gate or gates to section off that area.

- To confine your child to the bathroom. If—being the strong-willed parent you are—you decide to defy my authority and put the potty in the bathroom, using the potty bell becomes all but essential. You may also find that because the bathroom is unquestionably the most boring place in the house besides the coat closet, your child won't stay in the bathroom long enough to produce anything. To prevent a power struggle from developing, with you trying to keep your child in the single most boring place in the house and your child trying his best to escape, use the gate. When the potty bell rings, direct him to the bathroom and close the gate. Tell him to call you when he has something to show you and walk away. To lessen his boredom, put a few books and toys in the bathroom so he has something besides cold porcelain to keep him company. Under the circumstances, it is not important that he sit on the potty while he's in the bathroom; it's only important that he stay in there, with his potty, until he feels the urge. Then he can sit and release and call you and show you and get out of there. Freedom is a great reinforcer of proper behavior, by the way, so this probably won't take long. There is a possibility, however small, that your child will stay in the bathroom without a gate. Give that a try. If it's obvious after one or two attempts that he's not going to stay, then go to the gate.

In either case, using a gate will help you avoid micromanagement (which can express itself in a variety of ways, from pleading and bribing to threatening and using physical force) and can also be an effective way of gently enforcing compliance with the new rule.

Some children, and especially those who are confined in the bathroom, may be extremely unhappy with the gate. They stand at the gate and scream to be released. If that happens with your child, keep in mind that being so confined is not doing your child psychological harm. He just doesn't like it. If that happens and his screaming doesn't lessen after a couple of days, then it's time for the Doctor to make an appearance.

As calmly as possible, with a hint of cheeriness, say, "Sweetheart, the doctor says when the potty bell rings, you have to go into the bathroom and use the potty, and he says I have to put up the gate. When you make something in your potty, call me!" And walk away. If the screaming continues, come back after five or ten minutes and give him the message again. The older the child, the more complaint you're going to get, and the longer the gate is going to be necessary. An eighteen-month-old may protest for ten minutes; a three-year-old may protest for an hour or more. Hang in there! Good things come to those who gate!

Continue using the gate until your child is going to the bathroom independently when the potty bell rings, and continue using the bell until your child is going to the bathroom without that cue. If you use the gate for a couple of weeks, things seem to be going reasonably well, and you want to see what happens without the gate, fine. However, do not hesitate to bring the gate back into play at the first sign of resistance or disinterest. The occasional child even likes the gate because of the structure (and therefore security) it provides. For example, one little girl of twenty-one months, who hated the gate at first, ended up asking her mother for it! Just the same, your child will let you know, one way or another, when he doesn't need the gate anymore.

For any reader who needs some real-life inspiration, here's a true story from a mom who was right on the edge of cerebral meltdown when she got in touch with me through the members' side of my Web site. She reported that her twenty-seven-month-old son was into day six of

N75 and making ZERO (her word, her capitals) progress. Complicating matters, her husband was in the military, serving in Iraq, and she was six months pregnant with her second child. She had her belly and her hands full! In her first communication to me, she wrote:

Q *I'm using the potty bell, he wears thin cotton underwear, and the potty is in the living room because that's where we spend most of our time. He hasn't gone in the potty even once. Every time he goes (on the floor, in the bathtub, on ME), I have him sit on the potty to "try to go more" and remind him casually that pee and poopy go in the potty, just like Mommy does. I haven't yelled or punished him. I'm not sure what I'm doing wrong, but tonight, in addition to peeing in the middle of the living room, he started jumping and playing in it, as if it were a rain puddle. Seriously, I wanted to laugh and scream all at the same time (I did neither, just directed him to his potty to "try to go more" and cleaned it up). I feel like he's further away from using the potty instead of closer. What am I doing wrong? What am I not doing? What else can I do?!*

A I told her it was time to use the gate and potty bell and described how to do so. Needless to say, I emphasized the need to stay calm and purposeful. Seven days later, she sent me this update:

Q *Woohoo! After about two weeks using N75, my twenty-seven-month-old son is using the potty chair without any prompting or assistance from me, and we even were able to stop using the gate and bell! It didn't look good at first, but following your advice and persevering really paid off! I still can't believe it. It took twelve days! And he's dry at night, too! He decided he liked his underwear and wanted to wear them to bed, so I let him. The last three nights he's gotten up, used his potty, and gone back to sleep! The biggest thing I've learned is that when your* *child realizes you mean what you say, it's smooth sailing! So to all parents struggling through the potty-training process, I want to say: Stick with it! You won't be sorry!*

A In twelve days, this mom went from complete desperation to complete success. As she points out, the secret was developing a plan, communicating her expectations clearly and confidently, and staying the course.

In the last two chapters we've covered all of the elements of N75. Now it's time to take them one step further, to the rehabilitation of older children who simply refuse to poop or pee in the proper place.

5

TOILET-TRAINING REHAB WITH AN OLDER CHILD

Fifty-plus years ago, it was rare to find a twenty-four-month-old child who was not toilet trained or at least most of the way there. Today, it's not unusual to find intelligent, capable children older than three who are still peeing and pooping on themselves. As both research and an abundance of anecdotes have confirmed, these kids are not easier to train because they are older; rather, because they are older, they are likely to be perfectly content soiling and wetting themselves and highly resistant to changing the status quo. Mind you, these are kids who know how to use the toilet. In almost every case, they've displayed that understanding on occasion. They simply refuse to use it. They're not having accidents; they're having "on purposes."

More often than not, by the time these kids are three, their parents have tried to persuade them to join the civilized world. On such occasions, these parents have interpreted the slightest show of resistance or incomprehension as meaning their kids aren't ready. Doing what Brazelton and others advise, they abandon the training attempt, then pick it back up several months later. At that point, their kids are even *more* likely to be resistant, so the attempt is again abandoned, and so on.

By the time these kids are three-and-one-half, their parents are on the edge of toilet-training-induced insanity. Some have even crossed the line. In the meantime, toilet training has evolved into a family soap opera. The combination of habit, learned laziness, and sitting center stage in the family can create a nightmarish situation in which the child in question is determined he's *not* going to use the toilet, no matter what.

If you are one of the many American parents now living this nightmare, take heart! I've already given you all the tools you need to solve your problems. As the parents in the following true-life examples discovered, all you need is a plan and the resolve to make it work.

PLAN AND RESOLVE: PART ONE

Some years ago, while flying from somewhere to somewhere else, my seatmate and I began talking. He asked what I did and I told him, upon which he began sharing with me some of the problems he and his wife were having with their four-year-old son, one of which was his refusal to use the toilet, as a consequence of which, he was still in diapers. He asked my advice.

I told him that he and his wife should first get rid of the diapers, pull-ups, and any other evidence of the problem. The child should walk around the house wearing only thin cotton pants (not absorbent training pants!) and a T-shirt until his education was complete. Meanwhile, they should pump him full of water. I emphasized water, as opposed to sugar-sweetened drinks, including fruit juice. A timer should be set to go off every hour, on the hour, at which time the child should be directed or taken to the bathroom and told he cannot come out until he has produced a significant amount of waste of one sort or another. Furthermore, I said, accidents should result in the child being sent to his room, which should be "cleansed" of his favorite playthings, and he is to wait until the potty bell next rings. In this instance, however, when he produces, he goes back to his room until the bell rings again. And so on. The father listened intently, but I wasn't sure whether he thought I was nuts or on to something.

A few months later, he sent me this e-mail: "You may remember sitting next to the dad who complained about his four-year-old son's toileting problems. You were so right about the 'cold turkey' thing.

To make a long story short, I spoke to my wife on the phone right after our flight and told her what you had said. That evening, while I was still away, she began the program. When the bell rang, she took him to the bathroom and told him he couldn't come out until he'd done something, and the something had to be more than just a 'piddle.' Meanwhile, she was pumping him full of water, as you had advised. She even told him that if he hadn't gone by bedtime, she'd put his sleeping bag in there. It took him four hours of standing in the bathroom with nothing to do before he gave in. Anyway, it worked, and he was incredibly proud of himself. He hasn't had a problem since. Amazing that something we'd struggled with for two years was over with in one night."

Please note, dear reader, that the "force" in question did not create a psychological problem; rather, it eliminated one.

PLAN AND RESOLVE: PART TWO

Greta was four-and-one-half when her mother got in touch with me and literally begged for help. She had first tried to toilet train her daughter at age two-and-one-half, but when success was not obtained in a few days, Mom put Greta back in diapers. Three months or so later, she tried again, and again, Greta didn't cooperate, and again Mom put her back in diapers. And so it went, every three months or so until Mom, nearly out of her mind, called me. At this point, Greta was telling her mother that she wasn't ever going to use the toilet. If that meant she couldn't go to kindergarten (she was scheduled to begin in four months), so be it.

"I'll just stay with Na-Na [her grandmother]," she announced.

Within a week of my first contact with her mother, Greta's toilet-training drama was a thing of the past. Actually, from the moment Greta's mother implemented the plan, it took three hours, and three simple steps, to bring about Greta's complete, permanent rehabilitation.

STEP ONE: SET THE STAGE. Mom sent Greta to stay with Na-Na one afternoon. During Greta's absence, Mom stripped her room of everything except her furniture. Her toys, books, and stuffed animals were boxed and taken to a small rental storage unit. Mom also got rid of everything associated with wearing diapers, including the diapers themselves, changing table, talcum powder, and anti-rash ointment. In preparation, Mom had gone out and bought Greta a dozen or so pairs of thin cotton panties and put a bucket of water in the bathroom.

STEP TWO: COMMUNICATE THE PLAN. When Greta came home from Na-Na's, Mom removed her diaper and helped her put on a pair of her new panties, informing her that the days of diapers were over for good.

Mom told Greta, "If you pee or poop in your new panties, you will go to the bathroom and wash them out yourself in the bucket that's in there, then you'll spend the rest of the day in your room. You can't come out except to use the bathroom. If you use the toilet correctly, you can stay out of your room for the rest of the day—unless you pee or poop on yourself again, that is."

Mom then showed Greta her room and told her she'd start getting her toys back, one every on-purpose-free day (beginning with her least-favorite toy and working up from there), when she began using the toilet. If she had a relapse, all of her toys would be confiscated, and she'd start over from square one.

STEP THREE: IMPLEMENT AND FOLLOW THROUGH. To show her disdain for the new plan, Greta promptly began screaming. Topping that, she peed on the floor, right in front of her mother. Mom calmly took her to the bathroom, put some liquid soap in the bucket of water, and left her alone to wash out her new panties. For fifteen minutes or so, Greta sat in the bathroom crying. When she figured out that Mom was serious, she washed out her panties and called to be released from quarantine. Mom led her to her room and told her to call out if she wanted to use the toilet.

Greta began crying and screaming as if she was being tortured. She screamed and cried and cried and screamed for more than two hours. Then, she stopped and called out, sobbingly, "Mah-ha-me! I wah-hant to-hoo use the pah-ah-tee!"

Mom let Greta out of her room and directed her to the bathroom. Greta promptly peed and pooped in the toilet and never peed or pooped on herself ever again. Ta-da!

Amazing? Not at all. Simply a testament to something parents knew before common sense was smothered by psychological theory: A misbehaving, disruptive child cannot be coaxed into behaving properly. Rather, she must be *compelled* to behave properly by parents who are willing to make her temporarily unhappy.

It is ironic indeed that in order to equip a child with the skills needed to pursue happiness, her parents must see to it that she is familiar with unhappiness. Not abject, unrelenting misery, mind you, but the anger or grief that accompanies the startling, sobering realization that your feelings are not what makes the world go 'round, that you are not enthroned at the center of the universe, that the *mono* in *monotheism* is not you.

PLAN AND RESOLVE: PART THREE

The mother of a three-and-one-half-year-old boy wrote to me complaining that he was, in professional lingo, a "stool refuser." He held and held and held some more. Then he'd beg for a diaper, which his very exasperated and concerned mother would put on him, at which time he would stand in front of her, bend over slightly, get red in the face, grunt, and poop. Nice, eh?

First, I pointed out that Prince Constipatus obviously had mastery of his bowel movements. His constipation was self-induced, not the result of a physical problem. (I also told her that if she had any doubts about that, she should consult her pediatrician.) Holding was actually a form of rebellion. He was determined that his bowel movements were going to take place on *his* terms, no one else's. Both literally and figuratively, this was a *control* issue.

With that in mind, I recommended that she tell him that she had spoken to a doctor who helped children who didn't want to poop in the potty, and that this doctor had instructed her to gate him in the bathroom with a few of his favorite toys and books.

She told him, "The doctor says I have to put you in there in the morning, right after breakfast, and you have to stay there until you poop in the potty. I can't stay with you. I can't read to you or play with you in there. The doctor says so. I have to leave you alone so you can think about pooping."

Following the doctor's orders, the parents began Prince Constipatus's rehabilitation on a Saturday. They allowed him out of the bathroom to eat, take naps, and go to bed in the evening. That weekend, a parent was always at home with him. It took nearly two full days. Sunday, late in the afternoon, the parents heard him calling from the bathroom: "I poopy! I poopy!" They went back to inspect, and sure enough, there it was in all its olfactory glory.

The next day, Monday, Mom asked him, "Do you need to go back in the bathroom today?" He said he didn't, but by midafternoon, Mom could see that another dose of the gate was needed to loosen things up. Twenty minutes later, he began the poopy chant. The gate was used sporadically over the next few weeks, at which time Prince Constipatus officially became Prince Regularitus, and that was that.

The manner in which these parents solved this toilet-training problem with their son can be applied to a broad range of disciplinary situations. They told him, clearly and authoritatively, what they expected, told him what the consequences were of noncompliance, and followed through precisely as described. This is not rocket science.

I could regale the reader with countless similar success stories parents have shared with me over the years, but they would simply give redundant proof to what I hope I've already sufficiently proven:

- Toilet training is no more of a big deal than teaching a child how to feed himself.

- If it is introduced to a child during its proper season—between eighteen and twenty-four months—and introduced authoritatively as opposed to beseechingly, the child will learn this simple skill quickly and proudly.

- When children of proper age resist or seem oblivious to using the potty, the most common cause of the problem is not a lack of readiness but rather parental anxiety and attendant parental micromanagement.

- Even children who have resisted using the potty for years can be rehabilitated fairly quickly.

Lastly, let me remind the reader that none of what I recommend is new. I hope I have succeeded at convincing you that where children are concerned, "what is new is not true, and what is true is not new."

And now I'd like to give some parents a chance to ask questions. Let's begin with the lady in the back row dressed in the orange jumpsuit:

Q *Thank you! Our six-year-old wets himself during the day. This started at age four, shortly after the birth of a brother and a visit from female cousins. He has always wet at night, but that hasn't concerned us. We are at our wits' end with this daytime problem, however. He was completely trained at two years, six months, if that makes any difference. To deal with this problem, we've tried rewards (worked temporarily), loss of privileges, and punishment. A urologist examined him thoroughly and assured us there are no abnormalities; however, he said to be completely* *sure he needs to catheterize and run more tests. We're not willing to do this, and the urologist is not 100 percent for it, either. Help!*

A That may sound complicated, but it's really not. Let's take the two issues—bedwetting and wetting during the day—one at a time.

By age six, a small number of boys (and a very, very small number of girls) are still wetting the bed. At this age, a bedwetting alarm is most definitely called for. With a child this age, the cure should take place within a month. For more information about this handy-dandy device, see Chapter 7.

The wetting during the day is a horse of a different color. That's going to require a disciplinary solution. When the bedwetting has stopped for at least a month, tell your son that his doctor has said that wetting during the day is a sign of not getting enough sleep. Therefore, until the wetting has stopped completely for three weeks, his doctor says that he has to go to bed, lights out, two hours earlier every night. No child I've ever known wants to go to bed early. The problem should be solved within a month. Next question?

Q *Our six-year-old son still will not poop in the toilet. He has had problems with occasional constipation since he was in nursery school, but several exams have failed to reveal any medical problem. Now he will use the toilet to tinkle, but he wears a pull-up so he can poop, and will only do this at home. Any advice on what we should do?*

A Question: Who gives your son a pull-up? Answer: You do. Inescapable conclusion: As long as you provide this alternative, he has no reason to use the toilet. (As for medical exams, they certainly should be performed in cases of this sort, but my pediatric consultants tell me that they rarely reveal a physical problem.)

You've told me enough to know that your son's poopiness is most definitely within his control. He does not have "on purposes" (they do not qualify as accidents) at school, and his bowel movements do not suddenly explode from his body to his shock and surprise. He tells you he needs a pull-up, and you give him one (that's called enabling), and then he goes off somewhere and poops, and then you change him and help him clean himself.

The incidence of what pediatricians call "stool refusal" has increased dramatically as the average age of toilet training has increased well beyond twenty-four months. The problem rarely is seen in children who are toilet trained before their second birthdays. I suspect some of the increase is due to the fact that whereas pre-1960s parents usually bowel trained before bladder training, modern parents have reversed that sequence.

In any case, and as you might well imagine, as the frequency of stool withholding has increased, so has my experience with it. The solution is really quite simple: Tell your son, today, that you have decided he can no longer poop in pull-ups, period. Throw them away! Furthermore, if he soils his clothes, he has to hand wash them himself (first dunking them in the toilet and then finishing the process in a large bucket that you place in the bathroom) until they are clean enough to wear again. Make it very clear that you will under no circumstances put soiled clothing in the washing machine. After he finishes washing out his clothes, he spends the remainder of the day in his room (the entertainment value of which you should reduce significantly) and go to bed early.

FROM THE GREAT NEWS DEPARTMENT: Several months after I answered the above question through my syndicated newspaper column, the mother of said six-year-old gave me the following update:

Q *I wanted to write and let you know that I followed through successfully on your suggestion with my son (who was on-off with the pooping in his pants). When we instituted the "one month" without some of his favorite toys and sent him to his very boring room when he had an "on purpose" in his pants, he had only one incident two days after the month started. I showed him on the calendar what a month was. He got the message. Now he goes when he needs to go, and it's no big deal. Thank you kindly for the "kick in the pants" (no pun intended). I'm sure I'll be writing again, because we have to be one step ahead of him all the time to keep him humble.*

A I love stories with happy endings. Don't you? Okay, next question:

Q *My oldest son, soon to be eight, still soils his underwear during school or recess. Some of it is that he is embarrassed to use the toilet that's in the classroom, and some of it is that he gets busy and doesn't want to stop what he's doing. His doctor assures us that he has no physical problem. We have tried spanking, grounding, and threatening him with having to wear pull-ups (but we really don't want to humiliate him). We have even suggested that one of us might need to come to school and remind him to use the toilet. A counselor told us that our son's soiling was his way of expressing hostility toward us and suggested that we are too controlling. Is that psychobabble, or could there be something to it? Anyway, we'd sure appreciate some ideas.*

A As for whether the counselor's explanation qualifies as psychobabble, here is its definition: an explanation of human behavior that posits the existence of motives that cannot be verified by any objective means. You be the judge.

When an explanation of that sort concerns the problematic behavior of a child, the explanation always transfers responsibility for the problem from child to parents, thus paralyzing the parents' ability to discipline effectively. Quite simply, they no longer know who needs to be corrected: the child or themselves. In this regard, let's get one thing clear: This problem is of your son's making, not yours. Therefore, the discipline needs to be directed at him, not you.

Moving right along, the following is a disciplinary axiom: The manner in which parents define a child's behavior problem will determine the effectiveness of their approach. At present, you are defining your son's soiling in a way that gives him permission to continue in this bad habit. Saying he's embarrassed to use the bathroom at school or he's too busy to tend to business during recess are ways of excusing the problem. In effect, you are unwittingly giving him permission to be irresponsible, and then you are becoming angry when he acts on your permission.

You first need to define the problem in a manner that assigns full responsibility to him. I suggest that you call the proverbial spade a spade and tell him that it's rude (the smell offends others) and irresponsible. If you pull your punches here, you won't make any headway.

Up until now, your frustration has been driving your response to the problem. You swing from being confused as to whether he can control the problem to being angry. Your attitude has to become one of calm, determined intolerance. In that regard, I'll share what I recently recommended to the parents of a nine-year-old who was also soiling at school. When soiling occurred, the child was removed from the classroom, and a parent was called to retrieve him and take him home. There, he was confined to his room for the remainder of the day and allowed to come out only to use the bathroom. Before this rehabilitation program began, his room was stripped of all entertainment. I call this "kicking the child out of the Garden of Eden." He could come out of his room only to use the bathroom. If soiling occurred two times or more during the school week, the child was confined to his room for the subsequent weekend. Two school days and one weekend in his room was all it took for him to resolve his anger toward his overcontrolling parents and begin using the toilet properly.

6

INFANT ELIMINATION TRAINING: FAD OR FABULOUS?

As I was writing this book, the major media stirred excitement over infant elimination training (IET, also known as elimination communication), which is the practice of training children as young as six months to signal their mothers when they are about to go, at which time their moms hold them over or help them sit on a toilet, potty, bucket, kitchen sink (no kidding), or some other receptacle into which they release. A few words about this latest parenting fad seem in order.

To begin with, the Bible—Ecclesiastes again—tells us there is nothing new under the sun, and this is one such example. Once upon a time, what now seems new was the norm. Keep in mind that the premodern mom had to improvise diapers, was highly motivated to make her child as independent of her as possible at the earliest possible age (because day-to-day domestic tasks took a lot more time and effort than the same tasks take today), and in many cases could rely on assistance from older children and even grandparents and other relatives who lived within shouting distance, if not in the same house or apartment building. To expect today's mom (or for her to expect herself) to accomplish today what moms one hundred years ago accomplished is to ignore significant lifestyle differences, all of which mitigate against the typical modern mom.

Nonetheless, as attested to by the several thousand mothers who have had success with the method, some modern moms are obviously managing to make IET work. However, getting it to work requires that a mother become highly attentive to her child's elimination habits for months, the actual number of which will vary from one child to another. Then, once a child is trained to give the proper signal and is releasing on his mother's cue, she must continue to devote significant time and energy to doing for her child what he cannot do for himself—getting in and out of his clothing, for instance—and will not be able to do for himself until he is well into his second year of life.

I don't want to give the impression that I am opposed to teaching infants to use the potty. I simply feel that it's very labor and time intensive, and question whether it's really worth the time and effort in the long run. Again, this is not a matter of readiness. Although twelve months is six months before my earliest recommended start time of eighteen months, I am also aware that a twelve-month-old is an intelligent human being capable of understanding (as long as the communication is kept brief and basic) and communicating. You cannot harm a child by starting to toilet train this young. However, the mother who attempts IET may ultimately find it to be overwhelming. For that reason, I simply advise that the decision not be made impulsively but with full appreciation of the pros and cons.

Of course, a mom cannot train an infant if she works outside the home or is for any other reason unable to devote herself to the project. If that's not the case, and she feels up to the task, then I say nothing ventured, nothing gained. If after several weeks Mom decides IET just isn't working or isn't for her, then she should simply stop. This is very different from starting and stopping toilet training after eighteen months.

EARLY IS NOT NECESSARILY TOO EARLY

Over the past ten years, I've received lots of IET success stories, such as the following, from a mother whose friend gave her an article on toilet training pre-twos that I had published on my Web site. Said mom was inspired to take a leap of faith with her ten-month-old daughter.

Q *We bought my daughter a small potty, and when she woke up, we put her right on it, and she seemed to know what to do! I was more than amazed. I had a book about teaching sign language to infants, and we taught her the sign for potty. We also taught her the "ahhh" sound for bowel movements, as suggested in the article, and she could already say "pee." My pediatrician is a gentleman from India, and he was quite pleased that we were doing this. At this writing, she does all of her business in the potty. We even stopped with diapers. I invested in several pads for her mattress and several extra sets of sheets, but we have not had to use them as often as I thought. I do have to be a bit involved, but that is to be expected at this age, after all. Nonetheless, after putting her on the potty, I walk away and leave her on her own. I've since learned that in some other countries, she might even be considered somewhat behind in her acquisition of this skill.*

A Just imagine how much money this mom is going to save on disposable diapers! Mind you, not all children are going to be as quick to catch on at ten months, but this mom's success should inspire more such leaps of faith.

Another mother told me she started toilet training with each of her five children around twelve months and that in every case, training was successfully culminated by eighteen months. She freely admitted that she had to first train *herself* to be cognizant of signals from her child that elimination was imminent.

It all began one morning when she discovered her seven-month-old had a clean diaper. She sat him on the potty and gave him a piece of toast, and he had a bowel movement.

"I learned his rhythms," she wrote. "He learned my vocabulary and earned our praises. He quickly grew to prefer dry, clean pants, and began letting me know when he had to go."

She and her husband praised, let him watch them using the toilet, and helped him when he signaled he needed help. By age eighteen months, he was standing to urinate! She followed the same plan with her other three children, with similar success.

Her experiences led this mom to conclude that successful toilet training is primarily a matter of proper communication. I agree with her. She's convinced that by starting training early, one increases the likelihood that the child will become quickly intolerant of his or her own messy diapers and, consequently, more cooperative. I have no argument with that.

She closes by writing, "Certainly not all children will be as cooperative as mine were, but I'll bet that many, if not most, would be if someone taught them the language, knew their routines, and cared enough to give them sufficient attention and praise."

That sounds like an excellent prescription for a lot of parenting matters.

NOT SO FAST!

Then there's the flip side of the coin. Another mother who started IET with her twelve-month-old daughter writes:

Q *We have made great progress on the potty seat except for one area—she won't go in it. She knows what it is, how to lift the lid and sit down, what poo-poo and pee-pee means, and is even starting to say it. She flushes the potty for me when I go, and says "bye-bye" to it. I put her in training pants during the day when I am home—soft cotton ones the pee goes right through. So far, all she has done is pee on the floor. I tell her what it is, and where she needs to go next time. I put her on the potty when I think she needs to go, but nothing. When I sit her on the potty, I read to her from her favorite books, run water in the tub, and even let her play with water in a cup. I have even poured water on her "area" in hopes of stimulating something, but still nothing. She is fifteen months old now, and I am starting to get a little frustrated with this process. I'd appreciate any help you can give me.*

A The "help" I gave this mom was to advise her to stop, put her daughter back in diapers, and wait at least six months before starting N75 training. I think she expected too much too soon, and when her expectations weren't fulfilled, she began getting anxious and started micromanaging (reading, singing, pouring water on her daughter's genital area). At fifteen months, three months into the process, she had already established a negative precedent for toilet training that wasn't going away any time soon, hence my recommendation of a six-month breather. This mom probably should have stopped two weeks into the process, but one lives, and one learns. I only hope that at the end of her "toilet-training vacation," when she began using N75, she didn't fall back into her bad habits.

By the way, I fully realize that telling this mom to stop and wait six months before restarting may seem inconsistent with the "stay the course" position I staked out earlier in this book. However, we're talking apples and oranges. My recommendation to stay the course once you start applies to children eighteen months of age and older (I might even lower that to sixteen months in some cases). This was a special case, involving a much younger child, so an exception to the rule was appropriate.

IS IET WORTH THE EFFORT?

Promoters of IET point out that it's eco-friendly, whereas disposable diapers are most definitely not. That's true, and I'm all for eliminating the estimated 25 billion disposable diapers that end up in landfills yearly. However, I suspect that the IET movement is not driven primarily, or even largely, by environmental concerns. Even so, cloth diapers are eco-friendly, and typing "cloth diapers" into one's Internet search engine brings up dozens of mail-order (and in some cases, local) companies from which they can be obtained. The studies that have been done on cloth versus disposable diapers consistently find that children who wear cloth diapers train earlier—generally before age two—than kids who wear disposables. That doesn't mean there's something about cloth diapers that causes a child to master use of the toilet at an early age. It means that moms who use old-fashioned cloth diapers are also more likely to lean toward old-fashioned norms when it comes to training.

Unfortunately, a good number of today's moms are highly susceptible to the marketing of parenting fads that hold forth the promise of helping them "bond" more effectively with their children, and sure enough, IET promises exactly that. Never mind that "bonding" lacks empirical definition (hence my quotation marks), studies have failed to confirm the efficacy of most nouveau bonding techniques (e.g., sleeping with one's child), and children raised by mothers who are relaxed and casual when it comes to giving affection and attention are as happy, if not happier, than children of mothers who consciously (anxiously?) try to "bond." In today's Mommy Culture, however, the "bonder" is the Good Mommy. This, I suspect, is IET's primary hook.

Once upon a time, and not so very long ago, toilet training was simply and straightforwardly accomplished before a child's second birthday. Since then, psychobabble has transformed it into a big deal that arouses great anxiety in mothers and results in children as old as four still wearing "Little Depends." For some mothers, IET can reinforce the counterproductive notion that toilet training is a big deal.

Then there's the question of whether IET is really worth the effort. To illustrate the point, I'll share a fairly typical IET success story: A mom reported to me that shortly after she introduced her twelve-month-old daughter to a potty and showed her a sing-along video that showed several toddlers using one, her daughter began sitting and having success. She writes, "As far-fetched as this story sounds, I now believe it is easier to train them at this age than waiting. I am sure, with steady encouragement and gentle guidance, my daughter will be completely trained by eighteen months."

I have no argument with that prediction. Likewise, most of the moms who've reported success with IET tell me that they began around twelve months but that full independence didn't occur until their kids were around eighteen months of age, on average. That's six months of training. Toilet training an eighteen-month-old takes four weeks, on average. With that age child, neither constant vigilance nor a near-symbiotic relationship between mother and child is necessary. In fact, a mother can arrange an eighteen-month-old child's environment such that he needs very little help from her where toileting is concerned. I am not persuaded that IET is a viable alternative to this sensible, relaxed, and traditional way of going about this teaching.

One final note: The same T. Berry Brazelton who has steadfastly maintained that toilet training before age two is psychologically harmful, when asked by *The New York Times* for his take on IET, said he was "all for it." Ah, but then he reverted to form, proposing that children trained as infants might someday wake up and realize, "Hey, this wasn't up to me, this was up to my mommy, and I'm not going to put up with it," at which time, Brazelton suggested, they might begin withholding or engaging in some other equally rebellious act.[16]

I simply report. You decide.

7

NIGHT TRAINING (SO-CALLED) AND BEDWETTING

A mother asks when and how to night train her toddler, who was successfully toilet trained at age twenty-four months. Since then, she says, she has put him in pull-ups at night and for naps.

This mom's question reflects the widespread but very mistaken notion that just as it is possible to *teach* a child to use the potty during the day, it is possible to *teach* him to either hold through the night or get up during the night when he has to go. Predictably, parents who believe in the night-training myth withhold liquids after a certain time of day and then wake their children every three hours or so and drag them, literally, to the bathroom to pee. Said parents are then amazed when their kids, who managed to pee several hours before sunrise, wake up soaking wet. So they begin dehydrating their kids even earlier in the day and taking them to the toilet more often through the night, and still their kids wet the bed.

Because they aren't getting enough sleep, and therefore become unable to think straight, these parents become convinced that their kids are just being stubborn or lazy. At that point, they begin berating, belittling, threatening ("Santa doesn't bring toys to children who wet the bed!"), and punishing. They put them back in diapers, saying unfortunate things like, "If you're going to wet the bed like a baby, you're going to wear diapers at night like a baby." The upshot of all this drama is that the parents go slowly insane and their kids feel like miserable failures.

LET'S BE CLEAR: The term *night training* is a misnomer. A child cannot be "trained" to remain dry through the night; rather, he learns *not* to do so. When toilet training is accomplished by twenty-four months, most girls manage to remain consistently dry all night one to three months later; boys, two to six months later. There's not much parents can do to advance this timetable, but withholding liquids and taking children to the bathroom periodically through the night will accomplish nothing. In fact, they are counterproductive.

What is the goal here? It is for the child to remain dry through the night! Without waking up! People over age fifty have to get up once or twice a night to use the bathroom. Under normal circumstances—and normal circumstances include drinking all one wants to drink right up until bedtime—children are able to hold through the night and wake up dry.

Does it not make perfect sense that one does not help a child learn to sleep through the night (at least ten hours) without peeing on himself by waking the child every few hours and dragging him to the bathroom to pee?

"Come to think of it, John, when you put it that way, it does make perfect sense!"

Good, then we're making some progress here. Likewise, it makes perfect sense that one does not help a sleeping child learn to control a bladder that is partially or completely full of liquid by depriving the child of liquid for hours before bedtime. Right? Right!

Now that we've cleared those hurdles, let's move on to the issue of wearing a diaper or pull-ups at night. The feel of wearing a diaper (or any other bulky clothing around the pelvic area) is associated with permission to pee whenever the urge compels. That's why a child should not wear a diaper or anything that feels even remotely similar to a diaper during toilet training. For the same reason, wearing a diaper or anything that feels even remotely similar to a diaper will prevent the child from learning to stay dry through the night. That makes perfect sense too, doesn't it? Yes, it does.

Now that we have dehydration, sleep deprivation, and diapers out of the way, let's move on to the mechanics of helping children develop nighttime bladder control.

But before we do that, here are a few words to the wise. It's vital to keep in mind that it's going to take anywhere from four weeks to six months for your child to train his bladder to sleep through the night with him. During this time, it is essential that no one get bent out of shape about the child's bedwetting. Keep in mind that wetting the bed has nothing to do with stubbornness or laziness. Think of learning to stay dry through the night as similar to learning to walk. A child does not simply, one day, get up and walk. He stands, teeters, falls, stumbles, falls, lurches, falls, and gradually, over time, learns to master the process. While a child is learning to walk, he falls. Is falling an act of stubbornness or an indication of laziness? Of course not! It is what it is. Likewise, bedwetting is what it is. It is no more cause for concern or parental frustration than a child falling when learning to walk. Some kids learn to walk sooner than others. Some kids stop wetting the bed earlier than others. Criticizing a child for falling will not help him learn to walk faster. And so it is with bedwetting.

Getting in a tizzy about bedwetting is nonproductive, but you don't have to be oblivious to it, either. As with daytime toilet training, parents can help a child learn to hold his bladder through the night by setting the stage properly, communicating expectations effectively, and responding supportively to mistakes, while always letting the child accept as much responsibility for those mistakes as he or she possibly can.

SET THE STAGE PROPERLY: To begin with, and until he's consistently dry for at least three weeks, the child should sleep without anything on below the waist. Needless to say, a rubber mattress cover is an essential item. Why naked? Because one cannot learn to stop making a mistake if feedback from the mistake is buffered.

The somewhat paradoxical operant principle is as follows: A child will learn to *not* wet the bed by wetting the bed. It is the discomfort of waking up in a near-puddle of liquid that causes the child to learn to hold until morning, which is accomplished "subconsciously."

Wearing any thick clothing around the pelvic area not only delays this learning but also contributes to the habit of releasing one's bladder as soon as it becomes uncomfortably full. In other words, the more reluctant parents are to simply let the child wet the bed and get over it, the longer the child is likely to wet the bed. Therefore, the child should sleep naked (T-shirt or pajama tops only).

COMMUNICATE EXPECTATIONS CLEARLY: Before you start, teach your child what to do when he wets the bed. Put him through the paces of getting up and putting a towel or towels over the wet area and then getting back in bed and going back to sleep. Believe me, a thirty-month-old is capable of doing this. The secret is patience and practice. When he's got it, you're ready to give it a go. Every night, you simply make sure there are a few dry towels by his bed, and as you tuck him in, remind him what he's supposed to do if he wakes up wet.

RESPOND PROPERLY TO MISTAKES: The first few nights, he will probably wake you up when he wets. Simply go with him into his room, remind him what he's supposed to do, and give him minimal help. In a week or so, he should be on his own, and in a couple of months, it will be all over.

In this scenario, I'm using typical time frames. However, although some children control their night wetting in a month, some take several months, and a few (mostly boys) wet the bed for several years. In the case of a child who is still wetting after age three-and-one-half, it's time to consider using a bedwetting alarm.

BEDWETTING ALARMS:
ONE OF THE BEST INVENTIONS EVER

To find one of these absolutely wonderful devices, simply type "bedwetting alarm" into your Internet search engine. Before you do, however, a few cautions are in order:

- First, expensive does not mean better. A vendor charging more than three hundred dollars is simply trying to capitalize on parental angst. Your pediatrician may also have access to an alarm system that she'd rather you use, so check with her first.

- Second, do not buy an alarm that involves having the child wear a special pair of underwear to bed. Buy what's called a "pad and bell" type. The pad goes under the bottom sheet and is connected to an alarm that sounds when the child begins urinating.

- Third, be prepared to help the child wake up to the alarm. Although the directions that come with most of these units are clear and simple, they usually fail to mention that a bedwetting child sleeps so deeply that he doesn't hear the alarm at first. So, for the first week at least, when the alarm sounds, the parents need to gently wake the child and put him through the paces: When he's fully awake, tell him to turn the alarm off. Then have him put a couple of towels over the wet area and get back in bed. Kiss him goodnight and leave. Eventually—it may take a few days, it may take a few weeks—the child begins hearing the alarm and waking up without his parents' help.

Upon waking, the child automatically shuts off his flow of urine. As time goes on, he wakes up sooner and sooner into his episode—and the wet spot gets smaller and smaller—until he eventually stops wetting the bed altogether. For reasons no one understands, instead of learning to get up and pee at the sensation of a full bladder, children trained by a bedwetting alarm just sleep through the night without peeing.

Because of the responsibility required of the child, I don't recommend bedwetting alarms for children under three-and-one-half, but some children aren't really ready for them until later. If parents begin using one with a child older than three-and-one-half but not yet four, and they don't see any signs of success within two or three weeks, then I advise suspending its use and waiting until age four to resume the program.

And now, I see that some folks are eager—bursting at the seams, even—to ask questions. Yes ma'am? Yes, you, in the pink poodle skirt.

Q *Thank you, thank you. Our thirty-two-month-old daughter has been daytime toilet trained since twenty-six months. At twenty-nine months, she started getting up once a night to use the potty, even though she went to sleep with a diaper on. Shortly thereafter, we began putting her in panties at night. Now, however, instead of waking once a night to use the potty, she wakes up several times. The good news is she's had only four nighttime accidents in the two months since the switch from diapers to panties. The bad news is she wants my help using the toilet two or three times during the night. I'm wondering if this will eventually take care of itself or if there's something I can do so I can begin getting a full night's sleep again.*

A Yes, there most certainly is. Tonight, before bed, tell your very intelligent daughter that you spoke with the Doctor, and he said when she wakes up in the middle of the night she should use the potty on her own, without waking anyone. Put a "totty potty" (I just made that up! Write it down, folks!) in her room, and walk her through the procedure. Appeal to her vivacious sense of imagination, beginning with "pretend you're asleep and you need to use the potty." By the way, if she indicates that she'd rather use the "big potty," fine and dandy. Walk her through the procedure that way then. Make an appeal to the "big girl" in her. Tell her the Doctor is very proud of her for not needing diapers at night any longer, and now he wants her to take the next step.

Then, if she still wakes you up, remind her what the Doctor wants her to do. If she resists, don't get into a conflict with her over this in the middle of the night. Just cooperate with her. The next night, remind her again what the Doctor wants her to do, and walk her through the "let's pretend" of it again. This may take awhile to sink in, but it shouldn't take more than a few weeks. Next?

Q *Our almost-three-year-old son has been potty trained for four or five months now. When he was daytime trained, he stopped wetting at night. A month ago he wet the bed a couple of times. A friend with older children advised us to spank, and one spanking stopped it. Then he started back to his preschool program. After the start of school, he started to wake us up every night around two o'clock. I finally told him if he got up again he would get a spanking. He stopped getting us up, but he started wetting the bed again. Now he's started back to preschool full time and is wetting the bed nearly every night. We have a nephew who is almost four who wets the bed every night. His parents were told by a therapist that it was a way of controlling them. Is that the issue?*

A First, the friend who told you to spank gave you very bad advice. That seemed to work, I know, but bedwetting is not a disciplinary issue. Second, the therapist who told your nephew's parents that bedwetting is a child's way of controlling his parents is wrong. Your nephew may be in control of the parent–child relationship (lots of kids are these days), but bedwetting is not one of his weapons.

Wetting the bed at thirty-six months of age is no cause for concern. The mere fact that your son was dry at night for a few months after he was toilet trained doesn't mean he can control his bedwetting now. No one knows why, but boys have more of a struggle with this than girls. By age four, for every girl who is still wetting the bed, there are four boys. Furthermore, it's not unusual for a child—a boy, usually—to be dry at night until age four or five and suddenly, inexplicably, begin wetting the bed.

Punishing the problem will not correct it, and may well make matters worse—much worse, in fact. A change in routine or a transition to a different setting often precedes the start of bedwetting. Your son started wetting, not coincidentally, shortly after he started school. Being in school during the day may wear him out. On one hand, that's good. On the other, he sleeps more deeply than before, and has started wetting the bed as a consequence.

If you are able to concern yourself with more important things and let time take its course, this little glitch will probably resolve itself within several months. If your son is still wetting six months from now, then consider a bedwetting alarm, described earlier in this chapter. In the meantime, stop threatening, spanking, and scolding and let nature take its course.

And our final question comes from the woman in the back who's jumping up and down, pumping her arm in the air, screaming "Me! Me! Pick me!"

Q *Oh, thank you, John! Six weeks ago, we got rid of the diapers and starting having our three-and-one-half-year-old son go to bed naked from waist down each night. He continues to wet the bed every night but sleeps right through it. We don't scold him for it, and he helps me strip his bed every morning. This means I do an extra load of laundry a day, which would be fine if I felt we were getting somewhere. My husband thinks he's not motivated. I think maybe he's not developmentally ready because he seems disappointed at himself and proud of putting lots of pee in the potty in the morning.*

A There's no such thing as a three-and-one-half-year-old being "motivated" to stop wetting the bed. Nor is developmental readiness the issue. As you've already noticed, bedwetting in a child this age and older—assuming toilet training was accomplished by twenty-four months—is associated with extremely sound sleep.

Your son might be old enough for a bedwetting alarm. Then again, he might not. In either case, there's no harm in trying one of them out and seeing whether any progress is made.

In the meantime, resign yourself to the inconvenience of washing an extra load of sheets a day for a while. It may help to keep in mind that a century ago, a woman on the western frontier would have laughed out loud at the idea that all a mother has to do is wash an extra load of sheets every morning. Try gathering firewood every day, and count your blessings.

Okay, that just about wraps it up. I'm going to take up a few more minutes of your time, and then you can consider yourself an honor graduate of the John Rosemond Academy of Toilet-Training Success!

8

IN CONCLUSION

There you have it: the only toilet-training program ever put forth by a mental-health professional in the Post-Commonsensical Age that really works! Over more than a dozen years in which I've been recommending "Naked and $75," I have been blessed by feedback from hundreds of parents who have used it with eminent success and, in not a few cases, saved themselves from nervous breakdowns in the process. I'd be truly proud of myself if not for the fact that N75 is proof of the axiom that nothing new is true and nothing true is new.

As I keep reminding the reader, N75 is a very close approximation of how yesterday's mothers toilet trained their kids before the professional toilet-babblers began confusing the issue. In some cases, it's more than an approximation; it's a replica! In those halcyon days, before America's parents began believing that capital letters after one's name were the mark of an "expert" in child-rearing matters, children were toilet trained in a matter of days, before they reached their second birthdays, by mothers who cared not a whit about so-called readiness signs. The mothers were ready, and that was that! These women were denied positions of authority in society, but they were righteous in their authority over their children. They said "Jump!" and their kids responded, "How high?" So when they said, "You're learning to use the toilet today," their children said, "Yes, ma'am." Those were the days, all right. We're unlikely to ever retrieve them, but any mother (or father, for that matter) reading this book—you!—can bring about a retro-parenting revolution in your home in no time. It's just a matter of attitude, and it can begin with teaching your young child to put his pee and poop in the socially approved place. For you, the successful discipline of your child begins right there. For your child, good manners, which is all about respect for others, begins right there.

I'm hoping this book changes America's parenting culture, that it gives folks an appreciation for how fundamentally simple the raising of a child can be. Most of all, I hope that this book would have caused your great-grandmother to smile and nod her head.

Back to the future!

ENDNOTES

1. http://askdrsears.com/html/10/t106600.asp.

2. Ecclesiastes 1:9.

3. Sigmund Freud, "Character and Anal Erotism." *The Standard Edition of the Complete Psychological Works of Sigmund Freud*, Volume IX (1906–1908): *Jensen's "Gradiva" and Other Works*, 167–76. London: Hogarth Press, 1908.

4. Hans Eysenck, *The Decline and Fall of the Freudian Empire* (rev. ed.). Piscataway, NJ: Transaction Publishers, 2004.

5. Arnold Gesell and Frances Ilg, *Child Development: An Introduction to the Study of Human Growth*. New York: Harper & Brothers, 1949.

6. Benjamin Spock, *Baby and Child Care*. New York: Hawthorne Books, 1968.

7. Robert Sears, Eleanor Macoby, and Harry Levin, *Patterns of Child Rearing*. Stanford, CA: Stanford University Press, 1957.

8. "Toilet Training Guidelines: The Role of the Clinician in Toilet Training," *Pediatrics* 103 (6) (June 1999).

9. Bruce Taubman, "Toilet Training and Toileting Refusal for Stool Only," *Pediatrics* 99 (1) (January 1997).

10. E. Bakker, "Changes in Toilet Training of Children During the Last 60 Years: The Cause of an Increase in Lower Urinary Tract Dysfunction?" *BJU International* 86 (3) (August 2000).

11. Marten W. deVries and M. Rachel deVries, "Cultural Relativity of Toilet Training Readiness: A Perspective from East Africa," *Pediatrics* 60 (2) (August 1977).

12. http://askdrsears.com/html/10/t106600.asp.

13. Elizabeth Pantley, *The No-Cry Potty Training Solution.* New York: McGraw-Hill, 2006.

14. Erica Goode, "Two Experts Do Battle over Toilet Training," *The New York Times,* January 12, 1999.

15. Ecclesiastes 3:1.

16. Tina Kelley, "Toilet Training at Six Months? Better Take a Seat," *The New York Times,* October 9, 2005.